COLLECTED POEMS FOR CHILDREN

Ted Hughes (1930–1998) published numerous volumes of poetry and prose for adults and children from the late 1950s until his death. His first poetry for children, *Meet My Folks!*, was published in 1961 and subsequent books went on to win, among others, the Kurt Maschler Award, the Signal Prize for Poetry and the *Guardian* Children's Fiction Award. His classic story *The Iron Man* remains a bestseller and was made into an animated film, *The Iron Giant*, in 1999. Hughes was appointed Poet Laureate in 1984 and received the Order of Merit in 1998.

Raymond Briggs was born in Wimbledon Park, South London, in 1934, and has produced some of the most cherished and admired picture books of our time, including *Father Christmas*, *Fungus the Bogeyman*, *The Snowman*, *When the Wind Blows* and *Ethel and Ernest*. He has won numerous awards including the Kate Greenaway Medal for Illustration, the Children's Book of the Year Award and the British Book Awards' Best Illustrated Book of the Year.

# TED HUGHES
# Collected Poems for Children

*Illustrated by* RAYMOND BRIGGS

**ff**

*faber and faber*

First published in 2005
by Faber and Faber Limited
3 Queen Square London WC1N 3AU
This paperback edition first published in 2008

Photoset by RefineCatch Ltd, Bungay, Suffolk
Printed in England by T. J. International Ltd, Padstow, Cornwall

A CIP record for this book is available from the British Library

ISBN 978-0-571-21502-7

10 9 8 7 6 5 4 3 2

# Contents

# THE CAT AND THE CUCKOO

## MEET MY FOLKS!

NESSIE THE MANNERLESS MONSTER

MOON WHALES AND OTHER MOON POEMS

UNDER THE NORTH STAR

*

*from* WHAT IS THE TRUTH?

SEASON SONGS

# THE MERMAID'S PURSE

*The Mermaid's Purse*

## Seal

Where Ocean heaved
A breast of silk
And a black jag reef
Boiled into milk

There bobbed up a head
With eyes as wild
And wide and dark
As a famine child.

I thought, by the way
It stared at me,
It had lost its mother
In the sea.

## Gull

What yanks upward your line of sight –
Is it a clifftop, soaring kite?

Only a Blackback Gull
Giving your eye a pull.

## Gulls Aloft

Gulls are glanced from the lift
Of cliffing air
And left
Loitering in the descending drift,
Or tilt gradient and go
Down steep invisible clefts in the grain
Of air, blading against the blow,

Back-flip, wisp
Over the foam-galled green
Building seas, and they scissor
Tossed spray, shave sheen,
Wing-waltzing their shadows
Over the green hollows,

Or rise again in the wind's landward rush
And, hurdling the thundering bush,
With the stone wall flung in their faces,
Repeat their graces.

## Limpet

When big surf slams
His tower so hard
The Lighthouse-keeper's
Teeth are jarred

The Limpet laughs
Beneath her hat:
'There's nothing I love
So much as that!

'Huge seas of shock
That roar to knock me
Off my rocker
Rock me, rock me.'

## Mussel

When you prise
Her shells apart
To say Hello
The Mussel cries:
'I know! I know!
I confess
I am a mess.

But I'm all heart –
Heart that could not
Softer soften!

'An ugly girl,
But often, often
With a pearl.'

## Sea-anemone

For such a tender face
A touch is like a danger.
But the dance of my many arms
To the music of the sea
Brings many a friend to me.

None can resist my grace.
All fall for my charms.

Many a friend, many a stranger,
Many an enemy
Melts in my embrace.
I am anemone.

## Blenny

Ocean's huge hammer
Shatters itself
All to forge
This wiry wee elf.

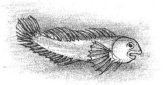

## Cormorant

Drowned fishermen come back
As famished cormorants
With bare and freezing webby toes
Instead of boots and pants.

You've a hook at the end of your nose
You shiver all the day
Trying to dry your oilskin pyjamas
Under the icy spray.

But worst – O worst of all –
The moment that you wish
For fried fish fingers in a flash
You're gagged with a frozen fish.

## Pebbles

Where blown spray falls
We are the stones.

Of lands that burst
From sleep and bowed
Like animals
To slake their thirst
Where waters flowed
We are the bones.

## Hermit Crab

The sea-bed's great –
But it's a plate.
Every fish
Watches this dish.

Just to be tough
Is not enough.
Some of the smart
Don't even start.

I stay in bed
With my house on my head,
Said the Hermit Crab,
Or go by cab.

# Wreck

The sailors prayed to come to land
And their good ship's wreck soon made it,
And sat on the rocks like a one-man band
While the stormy sea still played it.

Now through many a winter's weathers
Many a summer hour
Under the cliff there blooms and withers
The sea's rare rust-flower.

# Jellyfish

When my chandelier
Waltzes pulsing near
Let the swimmer fear.

Beached and bare
I'm less of a scare
But I don't care.

Though I look like a slob
It's a delicate job
Being just a blob.

# Crab

In the low tide pools
I pack myself like
A handy pocket
Chest of tools.

But as the tide fills
Dancing I go
Under lifted veils
Tiptoe, tiptoe.

7

And with pliers and pincers
Repair and remake
The daintier dancers
The breakers break.

## Mermaid

Call her a fish,
Call her a girl.
Call her the pearl

Of an oyster fresh
On its pearly dish

That the whole sea sips
With gurgly slurps
And sloppy lips.

## Ragworm

Ragworm once
Was all the rage.
But suddenly, see
This foolish age
Of fish is in.
Fashion of flounce,
Of scale and slime,
Of scoot and squirm
And gill and fin
Gorping like fools.

Let future time
Be soon unfurled.

Bring all such schools
To end of term.

Return the world
to me, the Worm.

## Sea Monster

Calm, empty sea
So soothes your eye
'Such peace!' you sigh –

Suddenly ME!

So huge, so near,
So really here,
Your stare goes dry
To see me come

So like a swan,
So slow, so high
You cannot cry

Already gone
Completely numb.

## Whelk

I wonder whether
Whelks can wish?
If I were a Whelk
I think I'd sulk
To be a fish.

Though anything other
Than a screw
Of rubbery chew,
A gurgle of goo
Going down a drain
Would be a gain.

## Lobster

This is the Lobster's song:
'Has anybody seen a
Heavy duty Knight
Dancing through the fight
Like a ballerina?
I was a thrilling sight!
Alas, not for long!

'It was the stupid sea,
The fumbling, mumbling sea,
The sea took me apart
And lost my clever wits
And lost my happy heart
And then jammed all the bits
Back together wrong.
Now I'm just a fright.
I don't know what to do.
I'm feeling pretty blue.'

## The Mermaid's Purse

The Mermaid's shriek
Made Ocean shake.

She'd opened her purse
For an Aspirin –
What a shock!
Out came a shark
With a great black fin
Hissing: 'Here's Nurse
And Surgeon in one
Great flashing grin!'

Now headache
And head have gone
Or she'd feel worse.

## Shell

The sea fills my ear
With sand and with fear.

You may wash out the sand
But never the sound
Of the ghost of the sea
That is haunting me.

## Octopus

'I am your bride,'
The Octopus cried.
'O jump from your vessel!
O dive with your muscle
Through Ocean's rough bustle!
Though I look like a tassel
Of hideous gristle,
A tussle of hassle,
I'm a bundle of charms.
O come, let us wrestle
With noses a-jostle!
You'll swoon in my arms
With a sigh like a whistle –'

And she waved her arms, waiting,
Her colours pulsating
Like strobe lights rotating,

Her huge eyes dilating . . .

## Heron

I am nothing
But a prayer
To catch a fish.
A hush of air –

A bloom of cloud
On a tilting stalk.
Over the water's face
I walk.

The little fishes
Tucked in under
Missing my flash
Sleep through my thunder.

## Shrimp

The Shrimp sings: 'The sea's
Ugliest weather
Merely preens
My glassy feather.

'I have the surf
As a rocking chair,
Combers to comb
My dainty hair,

'Though it's true my meat
Is a bit too sweet
And all who happen to meet me
Eat me.'

## Conger Eel

I am Conger
Out in the rough.
Long enough
But growing longer –
Thicker too.
A bit of a shock
At my cave-door
Beneath my rock.
But look at you –

You're not so thin.
As for my grin –
Your teeth are quite a
Good bit whiter
And eat more.

## Flounder

The Flounder sees
Through crooked eyes.
Through crooked lips
The Flounder cries:

'While other fish flee
In goggling fright
From horrors below
And to left and to right

'I lie here
With a lovely feeling
Flat on my back
And gaze at the ceiling.'

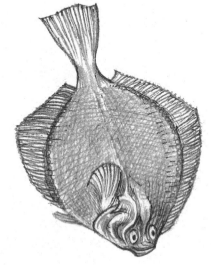

## Bladderwrack

The plastic rug
Of Bladderwrack
Upsets the sea
With its oily black.

No matter how
The breakers drub it,
And boil their lather
And wring it and scrub it

Its rubbery pods
Dry out on the shore
Tougher and grubbier
Than before.

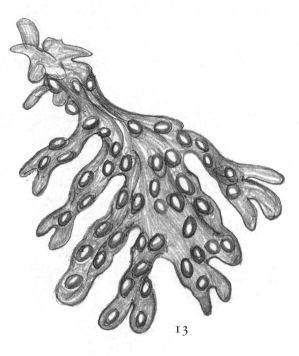

# Whale

O hear the Whale's
Colossal song!
Suppler than any
Soprano's tongue

And wild as a hand
Among harp strings
Plunging through all
The seas she sings.

# Sandflea

'O see my eyes!'
The Sandflea cries,
'So beautiful,
So blue, they make
The sea seem dull.'

But then she hides
Beneath the wrack.
She hears the tide's
Wild cry: 'Give back
That China blue
I lent to you,'
As it sweeps blind hands
Of scrabbling suds
Across the sands.

# Starfish

A Starfish stares
At stars that pour
Through depths of space
Without a shore.

She crimps her fingertips
And cries:
'If I could weep enough
Maybe
To rinse the salt
Out of my eyes
One of those dazzlers
Would be me!'

# THE CAT AND THE CUCKOO

# The Cat and the Cuckoo

## Cat

You need your Cat.
When you slump down
All tired and flat
With too much town

With too many lifts
Too many floors
Too many neon-lit
Corridors

Too many people
Telling you what
You just must do
And what you must not

With too much headache
Video glow
Too many answers
You never will know

Then stroke the Cat
That warms your knee
You'll find her purr
Is a battery

For into your hands
Will flow the powers
Of the beasts who ignore
These ways of ours

And you'll be refreshed
Through the Cat on your lap
With a Leopard's yawn
And a Tiger's nap.

# Toad

The Toad cries: 'First I was a thought.
Then that thought it grew a wart.
And the wart had thoughts
Which turned to warts.

'I tried to flee
This warty wart
With froggy jumps
But the wart got mumps.
Now this is me.
This lump of bumps
I have to be.

'My Consolation Prize
Is ten candlepower eyes.
But where are all the flies?
Eaten by those damned bats!'

His eyes pull down their hats.

# Thrush

The speckled Thrush
With a cheerful shout
Dips his beak in the dark
And lifts the sun out.

Then he calls to the Snails:
'God's here again!
Close your eyes for prayers
While I sing Amen.

'And after Amen
Rejoice! Rejoice!'

Then he scoops up some dew
And washes his voice.

## Goat

Bones. Belly. Bag.
All ridge, all sag.
Lumps of torn hair.
Glued here and there.

What else am I
With my wicked eye?

Though nobly born
With a lofty nose
I'm as happy with the Thorn
As I am with the Rose.

## Fantails

Up on the roof the Fantail Pigeons dream
Of dollops of curled cream.

At every morning window their soft voices
Comfort all the bedrooms with caresses.

'Peace, peace, peace,' through the day
The Fantails hum and murmur and pray.

Like a dream, where resting angels crowded
The roof-slope, that has not quite faded.

When they clatter up, and veer, and soar in a ring
It's as if the house suddenly sang something.

The cats of the house, purring on lap and knee,
Dig their claws and scowl with jealousy.

## Pig

I am the Pig.

I saw in my sleep
A dreadful egg.

What a thing to have seen!
And what can it mean

That the Sun's red eye
Which seems to fry
In the dawn sky
So frightens me?

Why should that be?
The meaning is deep.

Upward at these
Hard mysteries

A humble hog
I gape agog.

## Mole

I am the Mole.
Not easy to know.
Wherever I go
I travel by hole.

My hill-making hand
Is the best of me.
As a seal under sea
I swim under land.

My nose hunts bright
As a beam of light.
With the prick of a pin
My eyes were put in.

Your Telly's there.
You feast as you stare.
Worms are my diet.
In dark and in quiet

I don't eat alone.
At my table sit
Centurion
And Ancient Brit.

## Dog

Asleep he wheezes at his ease.
He only wakes to scratch his fleas.

He hogs the fire, he bakes his head
As if it were a loaf of bread.

He's just a sack of snoring dog.
You can lug him like a log.

You can roll him with your foot.
He'll stay snoring where he's put.

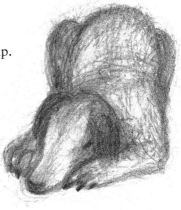

Take him out for exercise
He'll roll in cowclap up to his eyes.

He will not race, he will not romp.
He saves his strength for gobble and chomp.

He'll work as hard as you could wish
Emptying the dinner dish.

Then flops flat, and digs down deep,
Like a miner, into sleep.

## Cow

The Cow comes home swinging
Her udder and singing:

'The dirt O the dirt
It does me no hurt.

'And a good splash of muck
Is a blessing of luck.

'O I splosh through the mud
But the breath of my cud

'Is sweeter than silk.
O I splush through manure

'But my heart stays pure
As a pitcher of milk.'

## Squirrel

With a rocketing rip
Squirrel will zip
Up a tree-bole
As if down a hole.

He jars to a stop
With tingling ears.
He has two gears:
Freeze and top.

Then up again, plucky
As a jockey
Galloping a Race-
Horse into space.

## Dragonfly

Now let's have another try
To love the giant Dragonfly.

Stand beside the peaceful water.
Next thing – a whispy, dry clatter

And he whizzes to a dead stop
In mid-air, and his eyes pop.

Snakey stripes, a snakey fright!
Does he sting? Does he bite?

Suddenly he's gone. Suddenly back. A
Scarey jumping cracker –

Here! Right here!
An inch from your ear!

Sizzling in the air
And giving you a stare

Out of the huge cockpit of his eyes –!

Now say: 'What a lovely surprise!'

## Robin

When wind brings more snow
To deepen deep snow

Robin busies his beak.
But the pickings are bleak.

He stands at your open door
Asking for more.

'Anything edible?'
He stares towards the table.

The cat can't believe
A bird could be so naïve.

Half-shut eye, wide ear
She prays: 'Let him come near!'

Then, with his flaming shirt
Telling him nothing can hurt,

And that he will always win,
Robin bounces in.

## Ram

When a Ram can't sleep
He doesn't count Sheep.

He blinks, blinks, blinks,
And he thinks, thinks, thinks

'How has it come to be
That I'm the only Me?

'I am, I am, I am
Since I was first a Lamb.

'But where was I before?'

Then he snores a gentle snore

And hears, deep in his sleep
A million, million Sheep

Each one bleating: 'Why
Am I the only I?'

## Otter

An Otter am I,
High and dry
Over the pebbles
See me hobble.
My water-bag wobbles
Until I spill
At the river sill
And flow away thin
As an empty skin
That dribbles bubbles.

Then I jut up my mutt,
All spikey with wet.
My moustaches bristle

As I mutter, or whistle:
'Now what's the matter?'

(For that is my song.
Not very long.
There might be a better
Some wetter, wittier
Otter could utter.)

## Crow

Thrice, thrice, thrice, the coal-bright Crow
Baaarks – aaarks – aaarks, like a match being struck
To look for trouble.

    'Hear ye the Preacher:
    Nature to Nature
    Returns each creature.'

The Crow lifts a claw –
A crucifix
Of burnt matchsticks.

    'I am the Priest.
    For my daily bread
    I nurse the dead.'

The monkish Crow
Ruffles his cloak
Like a burnt bible.

    'At my humble feast
    I am happy to drink
    Whatever you think.'

Then the Crow
Laughs through his hacker
And grows blacker.

## Hen

Dowdy the Hen
Has nothing to do
But peer and peck, and peck and peer
At nothing.

Sometimes a couple of scratches to right
Sometimes a couple of scratches to left
And sometimes a head-up, red-rimmed stare
At nothing.

O Hen in your pen, O Hen, O when
Will something happen?
Nothing to do but brood on her nest
And wish.

Wish? Wish? What shall she wish for?
Stealthy fingers
Under her bum.
An egg on your dish.

## Pike

I am the Pike.
O you who walk
On two legs and talk
Do not know what I'm like.

You think I'm a cruel
Robot shark
Grabbing fish in the dark
To be my fuel.

No, no! I laze
Through the blazing June days.

On, on, all Summer
I sunbathe in bliss
And gaze at the sky

And pray to become a
Dragonfly.

Remember this
When you say that my fangs
Are solid hunger-pangs,
And that my work
Is murder in the murk,
And that I draw my wages
In the Dark Ages.

## Sparrow

Sparrow squats in the dust
Begging for a crust.

'Help an old soldier,' he cries.
He doesn't care if he lies.

All he wears on his back
Is a raggy sack.

All day the same old shout:
'I'm back from the wars, worn out!'

Though it looks like shirking
He works at it like working.

Later, on the chimney pot
He takes his sauna very hot.

## The Red Admiral

This butterfly
Was the ribbon tie

On the Paradise box
Of Paradise chocs.

O where's the girl
Who wouldn't go bare

29

As a thistle to wear
Such a bow in her hair.

## Shrew

Shrill and astonishing the shrew
Dashes through the early dew.

He's a famine on four feet:
'Something to eat! Something to eat!'

His scream is thinner than a pin
And hurts your ear when it goes in.

And when he meets another shrew
He doesn't rear on hinder toes

And nose to tender, waggling nose
Gently ask: 'How do you do?'

He draws a single, furious breath
And fights the other to the death.

## Owl

Owl! Owl!
A merry lad!
When he thinks 'Good!'
It comes out 'Bad!'

The poor Mouse cries:
'Please let me go!'
And Owl thinks 'Yes'
But it comes out 'No!'

OH NO! OH NO!
OH NO! OH NO!
HO HO! HO HO!
HO HO! HO HO!

'O rest your head,
You silly fellow,
Upon this lovely
Feather Pillow!'

## Stickleback

The Stickleback's a spikey chap,
    Worse than a bit of briar.
Hungry Pike would sooner swallow
    Embers from a fire.

The Stickleback is fearless in
    The way he loves his wife.
Every minute of the day
    He guards her with his life.

She, like him, is dressed to kill
    In stiff and steely prickles,
And when they kiss, there bubbles up
    The laughter of the tickles.

## Donkey

The Horse on giant, steely springs
Bounds all over the place.
It circles and circles and circles the globe
In an endless, panting race.

But the Donkey's huge strength
Is already here
At the end of the Horse's journeys,
Asleep, drooping one ear.

## Worm

Lowly, slowly,
A pink, wet worm
Sings in the rain:
'O see me squirm

'Along the path.
I warp and wind.
I'm searching hard.
If I could find

'My elbow, my hair,
My hat, my shoe,
I'd look as pretty
As you, and you.'

## Hedgehog

The Hedgehog has Itchy the Hedgehog to hug
And a hedgehog bug has a hedgehog bug.

Hedgehog with Hedgehog is happy at ease
And Hedgehogs with fleas, and fleas with fleas.

The batch of the Flea's eggs hatch in the crutch
Of the Hedgehog's armpit, a hot, rich hutch.

The Hedgehog's clutch of hoglets come
In the niche of a ditch, from the Hedgepig's tum.

And so they enjoy their mutual joke
With a pricklety itch and a scratchety poke.

## Cuckoo

The Cuckoo's the crookedest, wickedest bird.
His song has two notes, but only one word.

He says to the Linnet: 'Your eggs look so ill!
Now I am the Doctor, and here is my pill.'

Within that pill, the Cuckoo-child
Crouches hidden, wicked and wild.

He bursts his shell, and with weightlifter's legs
He flings from the nest the Linnet's eggs.

Then bawls to the Linnet: 'Look at me, Mam!
How quickly I've grown, and how hungry I am!'

She thinks he is hers, she is silly with joy.
She wears herself bare for the horrible boy.

Till one day he burps, with a pitiless laugh,
'I've had enough of this awful Caf!'

And away he whirls, to Cuckooland,
And leaves her to weep with a worm in her hand.

## Peacock

A perfect Peacock on the lawn
   Pranced proudly through his paces.
Pecked at old pancakes, flared his fan
   Like a hand of neon aces.

But while we smiled, he sidled in
   To the nursery flowerbed.
With quivering crown and scabby cheeks
   He pecked off every head.

He slept in the wood. His shawl of eyes
   Drooped to the woodland floor.
O much as we admired his plumes
   A Fox admired him more.

# Snail

With skin all wrinkled
Like a Whale
On a ribbon of sea
Comes the moonlit Snail.

The Cabbage murmurs:
'I feel something's wrong!'
The Snail says 'Shhh!
I am God's tongue.'

The Rose shrieks out:
'What's this? O what's this?'
The Snail says: 'Shhh!
I am God's kiss.'

So the whole garden
(Till stars fail)
Suffers the passion
Of the Snail.

# Horrible Song

The Crow is a wicked creature
   Crooked in every feature.
Beware, beware of the Crow!
When the bombs burst, he laughs, he shouts;
When guns go off, he roundabouts;
When the limbs start to fly and the blood starts to flow
   Ho Ho Ho
   He sings the Song of the Crow.

The Crow is a sudden creature
   Thievish in every feature.
Beware, beware of the Crow!
When the sweating farmers sleep
He levers the jewels from the heads of their sheep.
Die in a ditch, your own will go,
   Ho Ho Ho
   While he sings the Song of the Crow.

The Crow is a subtle creature
   Cunning in every feature.
Beware, beware of the Crow!
When sick folk tremble on their cots
He sucks their souls through the chimney pots,
They're dead and gone before they know,
   Ho Ho Ho
   And he sings the Song of the Crow.

The crow is a lusty creature
   Gleeful in every feature.
Beware, beware of the Crow!
If he can't get your liver, he'll find an old rat
Or highway hedgehog hammered flat,
Any old rubbish to make him grow,
   Ho Ho Ho
   While he sings the Song of the Crow.

The Crow is a hardy creature
   Fire-proof in every feature.

Beware, beware of the Crow!
When Mankind's blasted to kingdom come
The Crow will dance and hop and drum
And into an old thigh-bone he'll blow
  Ho Ho Ho
  Singing the Song of the Crow.

# MEET MY FOLKS!

I've heard so much about other folks' folks,
How somebody's Uncle told such jokes
The cat split laughing and had to be stitched,
How somebody's Aunt got so bewitched
She fried the kettle and washed the water
And spanked a letter and posted her daughter.
Other folks' folks get so well known,
And nobody knows about my own.

*Meet My Folks!*

## My Sister Jane

And I say nothing – no, not a word
About our Jane. Haven't you heard?
She's a bird, a bird, a bird, a bird.
Oh it never would do to let folks know
My sister's nothing but a great big crow.

Each day (we daren't send her to school)
She pulls on stockings of thick blue wool
To make her pin crow legs look right,
Then fits a wig of curls on tight,
And dark spectacles – a huge pair
To cover her very crowy stare.
Oh it never would do to let folks know
My sister's nothing but a great big crow.

When visitors come she sits upright
(With her wings and her tail tucked out of sight).
They think her queer but extremely polite.
Then when the visitors have gone
She whips out her wings and with her wig on
Whirls through the house at the height of your head –
Duck, duck, or she'll knock you dead.
Oh it never would do to let folks know
My sister's nothing but a great big crow.

At meals whatever she sees she'll stab it –
Because she's a crow and that's a crow habit.
My mother says 'Jane! Your manners! Please!'
Then she'll sit quietly on the cheese,
Or play the piano nicely by dancing on the keys –
Oh it never would do to let folks know
My sister's nothing but a great big crow.

## My Fairy Godmother

When I was born the Wicked Powers as usual were
    waiting.
One said: 'This boy will build with bricks already
    disintegrating.'
Another said: 'Sometimes his eye will be flat and sometimes
    round.'
Another: 'Like a razor will come every little sound.'

Another said: 'The earth for him will have such magnet
    strength
It will drag all things from his hold, and his own body at
    length.'
Another said: 'For him, the golden beauties that he grasps
Will turn one half to mist and one to biting poisonous
    asps.'

Another said: 'A misty rock is all this boy shall be.
He shall meet nothing but ships in distress and the wild,
    empty sea.'
Another: 'He shall be a ghost, and haunt the places of
    earth,
And all the stars shall mark his death as little as his birth.'

The Wicked Powers, the Wicked Powers, they crowded to
    have their say,
And all that day they said it, but at the end of day
My Fairy Godmother stood up, the one Power on my side:
Brighter than any dawning sun, whiter than any bride.

'You will need this,' she said to me, where I lay powerless.
Two sticks of sugar she gave me, lemon-flavoured if you
    please.
'These will save you everywhere, because because because
I stick them together and make them a ladder to lift you
    out of loss.
The ladder will change and change and change, just cling
    to it whatever –
It will twist and spiral, just you climb up it forever –

Climb this ladder, climb it, then the will of the Wicked
   Powers
Will dribble harmless off your heels, like the water of April
   showers.'
She said this and she gave me a thing too tiny for the eye
But with a smile I never shall forget until I die.

'Sail the wide sea,' she said, 'And cross the broad land,
But take this little ladder though you cannot understand.
And when your children come to the world, break off a
   piece for each.
It will grow whole for all of you and lift you from the reach
Of waiting Wicked Powers, and their stupidity.
This very, very tiny thing, so far too tiny to see –
This is the magic gift by which you shall remember me.'

She vanished and the Wicked Powers vanished and I grew,
And what I remember of that day I tell it here to you.

## My Grandpa

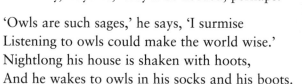

The truth of the matter, the truth of the matter –
As one who supplies us with hats is a Hatter,
As one who is known for his growls is a Growler –
My grandpa traps owls, yes, my grandpa's an Owler.

Though owls, alas, are quite out of fashion,
Grandpa keeps busy about his profession
And hoards every owl that falls to his traps:
'Someday,' says he, 'they'll be needed, perhaps.'

'Owls are such sages,' he says, 'I surmise
Listening to owls could make the world wise.'
Nightlong his house is shaken with hoots,
And he wakes to owls in his socks and his boots.

Owls, owls, nothing but owls,
The most fantastical of fowls:
White owls from the Arctic, black owls from the Tropic.
Some are far-sighted, others myopic.

There are owls on his picture frames, owls on his chairs,
Owls in dozens ranked on his stairs.
Eyes, eyes, rows of their eyes.
Some are big as collie dogs, some are thumb-size.

Deep into Africa, high into Tibet
He travels with his rubber mouse and wiry owl-net:
The rarest of owls, and the very most suspicious
Will pounce on the mouse and be tangled in the meshes.

'Whatever you could wish to know, an owl will surely
    know it,'
My grandpa says proudly. 'And how does he show it?
Sleeping and thinking and sleeping and thinking –
Letting a horrible hoot out and winking!'

## Grandma

My grandmother's a peaceful person, and she loves to sit.
But there never was a grandma who was such a one to
        knit.

Scarves, caps, suits, socks –
Her needles tick like fifty clocks
But not for you and not for me.
What makes her knit so busily?

All summer wasps toil tirelessly to earn their daily dinner,
Their black and yellow jerseys getting shabbier and thinner.

Grandma knows just how a wasp grows
Weary of its one suit of clothes.
She knits flowered skirts and speckled pants –
Now they can go to the beach or a dance.

Under the ice the goldfish hear December blizzards beating.
They have no fire at all down there, no rooms with central
        heating.

So when frost nips the lily roots
Grandma's knitting woolly suits –

Greens, blues, the goldfish adore them!
Winter-long they're thankful for them.

When snowy winds are slicing in through all the little
    crannies
The shrubs and birds in our neighbours' gardens envy
    those in my granny's.

    Her shrubs have scarves and pullovers,
    Her birds have ear-muffs over their ears,
    And cats that come asking for 'Titbits please'
    Go trotting away with little bootees.

A frosty Octopus received a stout eight-fingered mitten.
A Camel whose important hump tended to get frost-bitten

    Has a tea-cosy with tassels on it.
    A grass-snake has a sock with a bonnet.
    Folks can buy clothes at some shop or other.
    The creatures depend on my grandmother.

## My Other Granny

My Granny is an Octopus
    At the bottom of the sea,
And when she comes to supper
    She brings her family.

She chooses a wild wet windy night
    When the world rolls blind
As a boulder in the night-sea surf,
    And her family troops behind.

The sea-smell enters with them
    As they sidle and slither and spill
With their huge eyes and their tiny eyes
    And a dripping ocean-chill.

Some of her cousins are lobsters
    Some floppy jelly fish –

43

What would you be if your family tree
　　Grew out of such a dish?

Her brothers are crabs jointed and knobbed
　　With little pinhead eyes,
Their pincers crack the biscuits
　　And they bubble joyful cries.

Crayfish the size of ponies
　　Creak as they sip their milk.
My father stares in horror
　　At my mother's secret ilk.

They wave long whiplash antennae,
　　They sizzle and they squirt –
We smile and waggle our fingers back
　　Or grandma would be hurt.

'What's new, Ma?' my father asks,
　　'Down in the marvellous deep?'
Her face swells up, her eyes bulge huge
　　And she begins to weep.

She knots her sucker tentacles
　　And gapes like a nestling bird,
And her eyes flash, changing stations,
　　As she attempts a WORD –

Then out of her eyes there brim two drops
　　That plop into her saucer –
And that is all she manages,
　　And my Dad knows he can't force her.

And when they've gone, my ocean-folk,
　　No man could prove they came –
For the sea-tears in her saucer
　　And a man's tears are the same.

## My Brother Bert

Pets are the Hobby of my brother Bert.
He used to go to school with a Mouse in his shirt.

His Hobby it grew, as some hobbies will,
And grew and GREW and GREW until –

Oh don't breathe a word, pretend you haven't heard.
A simply appalling thing has occurred –

The very thought makes me iller and iller:
Bert's brought home a gigantic Gorilla!

If you think that's really not such a scare,
What if it quarrels with his Grizzly Bear?

You still think you could keep your head?
What if the Lion from under the bed

And the four Ostriches that deposit
Their football eggs in his bedroom closet

And the Aardvark out of his bottom drawer
All danced out and joined in the Roar?

What if the Pangolins were to caper
Out of their nests behind the wallpaper?

With the fifty sorts of Bats
That hang on his hatstand like old hats,

And out of a shoebox the excitable Platypus
Along with the Ocelot or Jungle-Cattypus?

The Wombat, the Dingo, the Gecko, the Grampus –
How they would shake the house with their Rumpus!

Not to forget the Bandicoot
Who would certainly peer from his battered old boot.

Why it could be a dreadful day,
And what Oh what would the neighbours say!

## My Aunt

You've heard how a green thumb
Makes flowers come
Quite without toil
Out of any old soil.

Well, my Aunt's thumbs were green.
At a touch, she had blooms
Of prize Chrysanthemums –
The grandest ever seen.

People from miles around
Came to see those flowers
And were truly astounded
By her unusual powers.

One day a little weed
Pushed up to drink and feed
Among the pampered flowers
At her water-can showers.

Day by day it grew
With ragged leaves and bristles
Till it was tall as me or you –
It was a King of Thistles.

'Prizes for flowers are easy,'
My Aunt said in her pride.
'But was there ever such a weed
The whole world wide?'

She watered it, she tended it,
It grew alarmingly.
As if I had offended it,
It bristled over me.

'Oh Aunt!' I cried. 'Beware of that!
I saw it eat a bird.'
She went on polishing its points
As if she hadn't heard.

'Oh Aunt!' I cried. 'It has a flower
Like a lion's beard –'
Too late! It was devouring her
Just as I had feared!

Her feet were waving in the air –
But I shall not proceed.
Here ends the story of my Aunt
And her ungrateful weed.

## My Aunt Flo

Horrible! Horrible! Horrible is my old Aunt Flo!
Yet very, very ordinary, I would have you know.
A tidy garden of roses, and a tiny tidy house.
She does not need a cat because there's nothing for a
        mouse.

        Nevertheless horribly nightly
        She goes straight up the chimney lightly
        Or through the wall, and not on a broom
        But astride a huge mushroom,
        A poisonous, red, white-spotted killer
        Grown on corpses in her cellar –

    She goes straight up about one hundred yards
    Then flattens out and aims for Scotland
    Or maybe Germany and as she goes
    She rips her false face off and reveals her true one
    Like a gigantic grasshopper.

My Aunt Flo's kindly smile is round and happy as an
        apple.
A bit of a girl in her day but now as proper as a chapel.
On Sunday in the choir her fine soprano can't be missed
Or at the Women's Institute the accomplished pianist.

        Nevertheless nightly her laughter
        Burrows in graveyards where she's after
        Dead bodies which she will boil

And render down for witch's oil –
Oil which she keeps in old gin bottles
For her supernatural battles.

A new-buried baby she will go three hundred miles for,
    it is a fact.
Its fingerbones for this, its toebones for that – horrible!
And men's dried features and women's vital parts hang
    in her attic
Dusty as dry herbs.

Her Sunday teas are cosy, with her cups so delicate.
A single crust-less sandwich of cucumber on your plate,
The crumb upon her smiling lip recovered daintily,
And after that a biscuit and another cup of tea.

But you never saw her where
She leaps at the moon in the shape of a hare,
Or bobs ahead of you or follows
In a weasel's shape, or wallows
Under the pleasure-cruiser's bows
In dolphin-shape, or reaches to browse

Your hair at midnight in the likeness of a donkey.
Did she pass your window, was that her?
A giant sow is already asleep in your bed, ten to one.
You saw her in the distance? Just a glance? For certain
You will wake up tonight with a frog in your mouth.

## My Uncle Dan

My Uncle Dan's an inventor, you may think that's very
    fine.
You may wish he was your Uncle instead of being mine –
If he wanted he could make a watch that bounces when it
    drops,
He could make a helicopter out of string and bottle tops
Or any really useful thing you can't get in the shops.
    But Uncle Dan has other ideas:
    The bottomless glass for ginger beers,

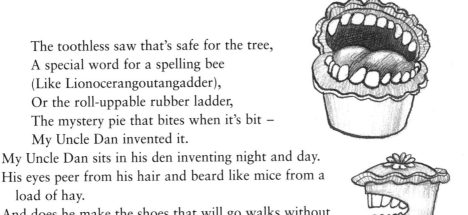

The toothless saw that's safe for the tree,
A special word for a spelling bee
(Like Lionocerangoutangadder),
Or the roll-uppable rubber ladder,
The mystery pie that bites when it's bit –
My Uncle Dan invented it.
My Uncle Dan sits in his den inventing night and day.
His eyes peer from his hair and beard like mice from a
load of hay.
And does he make the shoes that will go walks without
your feet?
A shrinker to shrink instantly the elephants you meet?
A carver that just carves from the air steaks cooked and
ready to eat?

No, no, he has other intentions –
Only perfectly useless inventions:
Glassless windows (they never break),
A medicine to cure the earthquake,
The unspillable screwed-down cup,
The stairs that go neither down nor up,
The door you simply paint on a wall –
Uncle Dan invented them all.

## My Uncle Mick

My Uncle Mick the portrait artist painted Nature's
Creatures.
Began with the Venus Fly-trap but he soon got on to
Leeches
Because he found inspiring beauty in their hideous features.

His portrait of the Lamprey, whose face is a living grave,
Knocked men cold with horror, made women quake and
rave.
'When you have seen what's what,' he said, 'That's how
you *should* behave.'

He painted a lifesize portrait of a laughing Alligator
With a man's feet sticking out, and titled 'THE CREATOR
DOING REPAIRS AND MAINTENANCE INSIDE HIS
EXCAVATOR'.

'The bigger the fright,' said Uncle Mick, 'The more it can
    inspire us.'
He filled his ceiling with the portrait of a vicious virus.
Out of his walls came sharks with jaws like doorways to
    devour us.

But alas his fate was waiting when he painted a tiger's roar.
We found his paints and brushes scattered round upon the
    floor.
Had the tiger got him? Uncle Mick was seen no more.

We gaze at the Tiger's portrait now. Was that my Uncle's
    fate?
His painting was too lifelike and his rescuers were too late.
Those eyes glare dumbly back at us and our hair stands up
    straight.

## My Mother

All mothers can serve up a bit of buttered toast,
Most mothers can handle a pie or a roast,
A few can boil a shark à la Barbary Coast,
But when I say mine can COOK – it's no boast.

When the Maharajah of old Srinagar
Wishes to make himself popular
Who can help him out but my Ma?
With elephant loads of nuts and suet,
With hundreds of coolies to trample through it
(To stir it you see), she produces a Cake
As huge as a palace that architects make –
Frosted and crusted with pink and blue icing.
Oh think of the knife they need for the slicing!

But special dishes are more to her wishes –
Nutritious, delicious, peculiar dishes –

Not just kippers in carrot juice,
But Buffalo Puff and Whipped-Cream Goose,
A Bouillabaisse out of no cook-book pages
With Whale and Walrus in collops and wedges
And festoons of Octopus over the edges.
(And should that give you the slightest uneasiness
There's Rose Crush topped with a peach's fleeciness.)

Sautéd Ant Eggs on Champagne Alligator
Are wonderful with a baked potato!
I took her a rattlesnake that had attacked us:
She served it up curried with Crème de la Cactus.

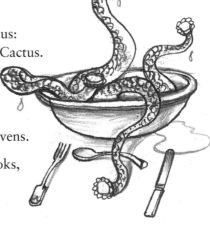

Her kitchen is a continual crisis,
Billowing clouds of aromas and spices –
Bubbling cauldrons and humming ovens,
Pans spitting by sixes, pots steaming by sevens.

Most mothers stick to their little cook-books,
But this is the way *my* Mother cooks!

## My Father

Some fathers work at the office, others work at the store,
Some operate great cranes and build up skyscrapers galore,
Some work in canning factories counting green peas into
    cans,
Some drive all night in huge and thundering removal vans.

> But mine has the strangest job of the lot.
> My Father's the Chief Inspector of – What?
> O don't tell the mice, don't tell the moles,
> My Father's the Chief Inspector of HOLES.

It's a work of the highest importance because you never
    know
What's in a hole, what fearful thing is creeping from below.
Perhaps it's a hole to the ocean and will soon gush water in
    tons,
Or maybe it leads to a vast cave full of gold and skeletons.

Though a hole might seem to have nothing but dirt
    in,
Somebody's simply got to make certain.
Caves in the mountain, clefts in the wall,
My father has to inspect them all.

That crack in the road looks harmless. My Father knows
    it's not.
The world may be breaking into two and starting at that
    spot.
Or maybe the world is a great egg, and we live on the
    shell,
And it's just beginning to split and hatch: you simply
    cannot tell.

If you see a crack, run to the phone, run!
My Father will know just what's to be done.
A rumbling hole, a silent hole,
My Father will soon have it under control.

Keeping a check on all these holes he hurries from morning
    to night.
There might be sounds of marching in one, or an eye
    shining bright.
A tentacle came groping from a hole that belonged to a
    mouse,
A floor collapsed and Chinamen swarmed up into the
    house.

A Hole's an unpredictable thing –
Nobody knows what a Hole might bring.
Caves in the mountain, clefts in the wall,
My Father has to inspect them all!


## My Own True Family

Once I crept in an oakwood – I was looking for a stag.
I met an old woman there – all knobbly stick and rag.
She said: 'I have your secret here inside my little bag.'

Then she began to cackle and I began to quake.
She opened up her little bag and I came twice awake –
Surrounded by a staring tribe and me tied to a stake.

They said: 'We are the oak-trees and your own true family.
We are chopped down, we are torn up, you do not blink
    an eye.
Unless you make a promise now – now you are going to
    die.

'Whenever you see an oak-tree felled, swear now you will
    plant two.
Unless you swear the black oak bark will wrinkle over you
And root you among the oaks where you were born but
    never grew.'

This was my dream beneath the boughs, the dream that
    altered me.
When I came out of the oakwood, back to human
    company,
My walk was the walk of a human child, but my heart was
    a tree.

# NESSIE THE MANNERLESS MONSTER

# Nessie

No, it is not an elephant or any such grasshopper.
It's shaped like a pop bottle with two huge eyes in the
    stopper.

But vast as a gasometer, unmanageably vast,
With wing-things like a whale for flying underwater
    fast.

It's me, me, me, the Monster of the Loch!
Would God I were a proper kind, a hippopot or croc!

Mislaid by the ages, I gloom here in the dark,
When I should be ruling Scotland from a throne in
    Regent's Park!

Once I was nobility – Diplodocus ruled the Isles!
Polyptychod came courting with his stunning ten-foot
    smiles.

Macroplat swore he'd carry me off before I was much
    older.
All his buddy-boys were by, grinning over his shoulder –

Leptoclid, Cryptocleidus, Triclid and Ichthyosteg –
Upstart Sauropterygs! But I took him down a peg –

I had a long bath in the Loch and waiting till I'd finished
He yawned himself to a fossil and his gang likewise
    diminished.

But now I can't come up for air without a load of
    trippers
Yelling: 'Look at the neck on it, and look at its hedge-
    clippers!

'Oh no, that's its mouth.' Then I can't decently dive
Without them sighing: 'Imagine! If *that* thing were alive!

'Why, we'd simply have to decamp, to Canada, and at the
    double!
It was luckily only a log, or the Loch-bed having a bubble.

'It was something it was nothing why whatever could it be
The ballooning hideosity we thought we seemed to see?'

Because I am so ugly that it's just incredible!
The biggest bag of haggis Scotland cannot swallow or sell!

Me, me, me, the Monster of the Loch!
Scotland's ugliest daughter, seven tons of poppycock!

Living here in my black mud bed the life of a snittery
   newty,
And never a zoologist a-swooning for my beauty!

O where's the bonnie laddie, so bold and so free,
Will drum me up to London and proclaim my pedigree?

## Nessie the Mannerless Monster

In Scotland is a Loch.
At the bottom of this Loch, in the pitch black,
A monster lives, called Nessie. It is just her luck.
She is about the size of a truck,
But shaped like an old sock,
With a long worm of a neck.
She is beginning to feel sick.
She is sick with sorrow. 'Nobody thinks I exist.
They all say my time has passed.
They say I am a fairy beast.
I do not want to boast,
But I will make myself known or bust.'

So Nessie rises in a great burst
Of spray, she smashes the water to mist,
She scuds around doing her worst.
But people just keep on driving past.
They say: 'No, No! Such things do not exist.'
Soon she grows tired and has to lie there, having a rest.

Then in a rage, she outs on to the road.
She says: 'I don't want to be rude,
But after all, I have my pride.'
She says: 'I am going to make a raid
On Edinburgh.' Then all the tourists cried
'What's that? What's that? Oh, Oh, let me hide!'
And they crashed their cars into the roadside.
They covered their eyes hoping the sight would fade.
But Nessie walked straight on, she paid no heed.

The Mayor of Edinburgh nearly had a fit
When he saw Nessie. 'Look at it! Look at it!'
He cried, and fainted right there on the spot.
But the police said, 'Whose is that huge cat?
It is blocking our traffic more than a bit.

Divert it south to London.' So that was that.
Nessie had not opened her mouth and she was out,
Tramping south towards London alone and on foot.

As she was tramping down through Northumberland
Up out of a ditch pops this fox-hound.
'Look!' he howls, 'A fox as long as a brass band!'
The other hounds come running up and all stare stunned.
Then Wow-wow-wow! they chase Nessie over the
    ploughed land,
And into a wood and out at the far end,
Then into a meadow and round with the cows and round.
'I'm no fox,' cries Nessie, but they can't understand.
She dives into and just fills up a duckpond.
The huntsmen gallop up. When they see Nessie making a
    stand

They turn away their horses and tuck their hounds under
Their arms and creep off home quaking with fear and no
    wonder,
Seeing Nessie there in the duckpond like a coal-black forty-
    foot gander.

She marches south into Yorkshire, the greatest shire.
'Now,' she says, 'I've heard there are honest folk here
Who will all cry "Nessie!" the minute I appear.'
But what does she find? The streets are all empty and bare.
Everybody sits indoors in front of the TV with a dead stare.

There is nothing in the streets but cats, dogs and the odd
    parked car.
She peers in at the windows and whistles but nobody can
    hear
For the TV and its laughter and uproar and gunfire.
There is no other sign of life in all Yorkshire anywhere,
Till she meets a little boy and he shouts: 'Hey, you. Get out
    of here.'

Next, travelling through the woods to avoid the cars
She meets Sir Mimms Culdimple Bagforkhumberly-parse.
'You'll stay to dine,' offers that gent, with a laugh, 'of
    course?'

And he rips off an utterly dumbfounding curse
That kills a big orange horsefly on the ear of a nearby
  horse.
Nessie devours partridges, pheasants, pigs' heads, pike and
  parts of hares.
She drinks whisky and wine until it pours out of her ears.
Then she snaps up the servants, the cook too in spite of his
  roars.
She swallows a settee for wadding, the whole item
  disappears,
And finishes off her host in one gulp, and says: 'That was a
  solid first course.'
And falls down on the carpet and without apology snores –
All of which proves she was completely without manners
  and a perfect monster.

Next, she came up with ten thousand people and then
  some.
They all marched packed together, with here and there a
  drum.
They carry banners with the words: 'Ban The Bomb.'
They are laughing and singing and Nessie thinks: 'Is this a
  party? Can I come?'
'Be our mascot,' they cry, 'O peaceful beast, beautiful and
  dumb.'
So Nessie marches along at the head of them.

She has no idea what it is all about
But all these people follow her with song and dance and
  shout.
'They are taking me to the Queen,' thinks Nessie,
'And the Duke of Edinburgh will say, "There's a Bonnie
  Lassie!"
Then I shall be all right, I shall have class,
And everybody will say, "Oh everybody knows Nessie,
  she's a grand lass."
And all these good people are bringing this to pass.'

But when they got to the heart of London and Trafalgar
  Square

Somehow everybody disappeared into thin air
Leaving hundreds of policemen yawning there.
Whenever she asked a policeman the way to the Queen, he
    politely directed her to the zoo.
And so she followed the policeman's finger, which is what
    people in London do.

When Nessie walked through the zoo fence
The gorilla burst his bars and fled into the far distance.
The keepers jumped clean out of their clothes at the
    first glance
And hid behind the tigers which stood in a dumb trance.
The wolves fell into a dead faint at once.
The elephants gave up all thoughts of defence.

The eagles went rigid and cried: 'We are only
    weathervanes.'
The snakes murmured: 'Take no notice of us, we are
    only vines.'
The tortoises pulled in their heads and legs and whispered:
    'We are stones.'
The lions lay still with eyes closed and tried to look like
    sand-dunes.
And Nessie wandered around saying: 'Are all these
    creatures Queens?'

Till up came the small mammal-house keeper, braver than
    the rest.
'We have no place,' he said, 'for your sort of beast.
Go to Kensington Museum, that would be best.
They have all your cousins there, prettily encased.
You can meet them all and have a real feast.'
'Thank you, thank you!' cried Nessie, 'I will do just as you
    suggest.
I was beginning to feel weary and depressed.
I never knew I had cousins. When they see me won't they
    be surprised.'

In Kensington Museum all the curators stared.
They stared at Nessie, they had never seen anything so
    weird.

'Where are these cousins of mine of whom I have heard?'
Asked Nessie, but everybody went on staring, nobody said
    a word.
'Where are they?' cried Nessie, 'They'll tell you I do truly
    exist,
And that I am not a fairy-beast and not a dream-beast.'
Then up spoke a world-famous scientist:
'Impostor! You are impossible! If you were extinct and no
    more
Indeed I would say you were a Plesiosaur.
We have plenty of the bones of that beast which in its day
    was not at all rare.
But all Plesiosaurs, say our books, have been dead a
    million year.
Yet you are alive. Look at you. So who knows what you
    are?
Go away and don't bother us here.'
Then they all hurried to their jobs and left Nessie alone in
    despair.

Nessie wandered sadly along High Street.
'Get a move on,' snarled all the taxi-drivers, leaning out.
A huge lorry bumped her backside with hoot after hoot.
Tourists gasped: 'Look, quick, another famous London
    sight.'
Londoners thought she was an advert, for a circus coming
    that night.
Policemen roared: 'Drive on the left, idiot, not the right.'
What with all the noise and crowds Nessie was in a great
    fright.

But all at once a voice from the crowd roared 'Ness!'
Her eyes popped when she heard her name, joy made her
    nearly delirious.
It was a wretched Scots writer of verses, Willis by name,
    and he was penniless,
But he knew a monster when he saw one, Oh yes.
'Nessie!' he cried, and he gave her flipper a great kiss.
She told him her woes and he cried: 'Alas! Alas! Alas!
We shall go without hesitation to the palace.

Let me ride and you run.' And so in no time they were off
    at a great pace.

When they galloped up to Buckingham Palace, guards
    barred the way.
'Dogs on a leash,' they ordered, and, 'No visitors today.'
So Willis cried: 'The Queen's greatest subject has
    something to say –
Nessie here is the Queen's greatest subject, I will have you
    know.'
But the guards just bristled their moustaches, and it was no
    go.

Whereupon Nessie simply ran over the guards and left
    them looking for their hats:
But then the Palace Army, which always waits,
The Palace Army which protects the Queen from all
    dangers and frights,
Did not stand staring like dumb mountain goats.
They barked commands, scampered to their posts, manned
    their guns, gloated through the gunsights,
And Nessie and Willis were at any moment about to be
    blown to bits.

'Stop, stop!' shouted Willis, 'Let's have a peace-talk.'
Then out on to her balcony the Queen came for a look,
Her crown on her head, her stoatskins over her arm, to see
    this freak.
At the sight of Nessie she uttered a strange croak,
But then, like a true Queen, most politely she spoke:
Saying: 'What do you want, for heaven's sake?'

Then Willis up and gave his speech on Nessie's
    behalf.
In no time at all he told how her times were so tough,
In no time at all he told the causes of her grief,
Living up there in Scotland, monstrous beyond belief.
And the Queen was touched with concern for this gigantic
    national waif.
Then the Duke made a joke, and the Queen gave a
    laugh:

'You shall be Vice-Regent of Scotland, Wales and Northern
    Ireland,' she said, 'For the rest of your life.'

And so it comes about that Nessie reigns in Loch Ness.
On Sundays all along the shores the people press,
The bands of the Coldstream Guards and Scottish Light
    Infantry play *en masse*.

Nessie cruises up and down with a coronet on her head.
She is delighted, she never had it so good.
And Willis is a Civil Servant, he sees that she's well fed,
And he's delighted too, he gets so well paid.

And what finer life can there be than living on the shores
    of a marvellous lake
With a pet monster, and doing as you like?
The scientists come in tribes, for a look.
Nessie invents stories about her ancestors and they write
    them all down in their book.
And whenever the Queen visits Scotland, she visits this
    Loch,
Then she and Nessie sit sipping tea and have a really good
    talk.

MOON WHALES
AND OTHER MOON POEMS

*Moon Whales and other Moon Poems*

## Moon-Whales

They plough through the moon stuff
Just under the surface
Lifting the moon's skin
Like a muscle
But so slowly it seems like a lasting mountain
Breathing so rarely it seems like a volcano
Leaving a hole blasted in the moon's skin

Sometimes they plunge deep
Under the moon's plains
Making their magnetic way
Through the moon's interior metals
Sending the astronaut's instruments scatty.

Their music is immense
Each note hundreds of years long
Each whole tune a moon-age

So they sing to each other unending songs
As unmoving they move their immovable masses

Their eyes closed ecstatic

## A Moon-Lily

Marvellously white is the moon-lily.
But that is not all, O no, not nearly.

When it has reached its full height
But before its swelling bud shows any white

You think you hear a ghost inside your house –
It whispers and titters, so it is not a mouse.

By next night it is a happy humming.
Now go look at your lily, you will see a split of white petal
   coming.

Next night it is a singing – very far
But very clear and sweet, and wherever you are

The voice is always in some other room.
Down in the garden, your lily is in bloom.

For days now, while your flower stands full and proud,
That strange lady's singing, gentle and happy, and never
   very loud,

Comes and goes in your house, and all night long.
Till one night – suddenly – weeping. Something is wrong!

And you know, down in your garden, before you go
The lily has started to fade, there is brown on her snow.

Then come nights of quiet sobbing, and no sleep for you,
Till your lily's withering is quite through.

## The Burrow Wolf

A kind of wolf lives in the moon's holes
Waiting for meteorites to score goals.

The meteorites come down blazing with velocity
And this wolf greets them with a huge grin of ferocity.

Whack to the back of his gullet go those glowing rocks
And the wolf's eyes start clean out of his head on
   eleven-inch stalks.

But only for a moment, then he smiles and swallows
And shuts his eyes as over the melt of marshmallows.

Rockets nosediving on to the moon for modern adventures
Will have to reckon with those abnormal dentures.

Many a spaceman in the years to come
Will be pestled with meteorites in that horny tum.

If he does not dive direct into those jaws
He may well wander in there after a short pause.

For over the moon general madness reigns –
Bad when the light waxes, worse when it wanes –

And he might lunatically mistake this wolf for his wife.
So the man in the moon ended *his* life.

## Moon-Mirror

In every moon-mirror lurks a danger.
Look in it – and there glances out some stranger
Who stares at you astounded and goes pale,
Probably gurgles dumbstruck, or utters a wail
And flees, as if he had met a ghost –
And the mirror once more is a hole of silver mist.

Another time you glance in it and see
Strange faces, crowding excitedly,
As if you were some monster on display
And they could look at you, having had to pay,
Through that small window, from which they are pushed
By other amazed faces, that stare, hushed.

Or washing your face, you look – and see your face
Instantly shouldered out of place
By crowds of stricken faces from long ago,
Faces full of pleading and woe,
Who reach hands toward you, crying dumb,
But are shoved aside by others who come
Crying out of the future, baby faces
Strong as giants, with Martian grimaces,
Trying to burst and scatter the mirror frame –
What if they *did* burst it? What if they came?

Banish them, quick, with an angry frown
And turn the mirror face-down.

## Moon-Thirst

Moon-thirst
Is the worst.

Moon-stroke
Makes you croak.

A mighty smite
Of Moonlight

Turns your playful soul
That played like a silly foal

Into a load
Of dark toad.

He squats under a rock
Like a stopped clock.

'A drink! O for a drink!'
He croaks, with dusty blink.

'Ah, how low I have sunk
Since the moon made me drunk!'

But then, with raptures in his eyes,
He sees the moon rise.

Once more, with awful lust,
He plods out into the dust.

## Moon-Theatre

Set the stage
With a teacup, a carving knife, a book open at any page,
A watch, a flower and a chair –
Then tap a drum and fix your eyes in a glassy stare.

Out of the teacup suddenly springs a princess
Fleeing from a battle. Brambles have torn her dress.
She is on a wild mountain. The carving knife

Gleams and an ogre appears, and chuckling he makes her
   his wife,
And carries her into the dark cave of the book
Which is almost hidden with leaves. Now look

Inside the cave the ogre's nine wives
With all their children and aged relatives
Squabble in unending bedlam. The ogre
Hopes for peace with his new wife and is eager
To keep her disguised in a wolfskin, calling her
His pet wolf, which they all avoid in fear.

So whenever he leaves the cave
She is a wolf, and she must howl and rave
To keep those murderous relatives out of her room.
But she is wretched, hers is a terrible doom.

Till she escapes and flees on her four wolf-legs.
The chair follows barking. In vain she begs
She is a princess, the chair is a whole pack
Of great-skulled gaunt-ribbed hounds on her track
Till she gets to the flower and he snatches her up
As if she were no more than a cuddly pup.
Then his sword, which a moment ago was a leaf,
Deprives all those savage hounds of life.

The corpses become the ogre and his tribe. The princess
And her flower-hero run in happiness
Toward the watch, which is a waiting express
That rushes them to a world where ogres cannot occur
And girls have to be girls, and boys boys, and he can
   marry her.

You applaud. You shut the book up,
Put the knife in the drawer, you sit in the chair, put the
   watch on your wrist and the flower in the cup.

## The Moon-Oak

The Moon-oak
Is a sort of vegetable hawk.

He carries the Moon in his feet
Because that is his meat.
He reaches his arms high through the starry night
And that is his great flight
Long ago begun –

He flies toward the Sun
Because that is his nest.
There he will rest
And there greet his mate
Who brings the Earth in her feet.

Then Earth and Moon will expire
Among their nestlings of fire.


## The Moon-Haggis

The moon-haggis has a crazy
Cruel hiccup, as it flees
Across rugged highlands and flat oozy
Lowlands like a bagpipe with knees.

It skirls and careens its passion
To the hag-thorn and to the crone-stone
And to the black loch without a fish in,
Droning its chanter and chanting its drone.

Till a wild highlander, deserting his bottle,
With dirk and with dag
Cuts its throttle
And eats its bag.

Then the moon in the sky
Lets a gurgling cry
And shrinks to the skin
That the haggis lived in.

# Moon-Wings

Unexpectedly descending things
Are these moon-wings.

Broad, soft, silent and white
And like a huge barn-owl's is their flight.

They veer and eddy and swoop,
They loop the alarming loop,

No head or limbs or body – just wings.
A pair pounces down on you and clings –

You feel them trying to grow
Into your shoulder blades, then they flap and you go

You go you go you go –
Where or which way you can never know.

High over goggling faces you are swung –
And just as unexpectedly suddenly flung

Down to the ground – after flying
Nine or ten miles without trying,

Then the wings just whirl off
With a sort of whiffling laugh.

# Visiting the Moon

I tried the bell-pull –
But what use is the silk-tassel tail of a white bull?

I went in, feeling watched.
But it hadn't hatched.

I climbed the stair
That died in the cellar.

I opened the little door –
Space sat smiling there.

I slipped into the attic
Just as it turned over and the sand started to pour back.

I looked into the mirror –
It escaped, leaving a big-eyed feather.

I looked into the inkwell
Which still hadn't set sail.

When I met her in the dark
She jabbed me with a bent hypodermic.

Was I juggling with hoops?
Was I hanging from a hook through my lips?

I woke up in the tower

And there the moon, molten silver in a great cauldron,
Was being poured
Through the eye of a needle

Spun onto bobbins and sold to poets
For sewing their eyelids together
So they can sing better.

## Moon-Shadow Beggars

Crossing the frontier from dark to light
You pass the shadows, some of which bite
Because they need your blood, some on one leg
Hobble beside you and merely beg.
You can't hear what it is they want you to give –
I'll tell you, it is the body in which you live.
They cling with fingers that have no strength,
They reach after you with arms of elastic length,
They screech, sob and suffer in a dreadful way.
Be resolute, pass them without delay.
For if you pity them, and pause, you will stay
Caught among them forever, they will pour
Into you through the wide open door
Of your eye-pupil, and fill you up

And you will be nothing but a skinful of shadows
Whispering shadow-talk and groping for
The well-known handle of your own front door
With fingers that cannot feel it.
It is a horrible state and nothing can heal it.

## The Earth-Owl

Far undergrounded,
Moon-miners dumbfounded
Hear the speed-whistle
Of this living missile
As he tears through the strata
Or splits apart a
Subterrene Gibraltar,
His wings do not falter
At deposits of iron –
He just screws a new eye on
The end of his skull
Which is shaped with great skill
As a terrible drill
That revolves on his neck –
His spine is the spindle,
His body the handle,
His wings are the thrust –
In a gunshot of dust
Sparks, splinters and all he
Bursts from the mine-wall,
Shrieking 'Ek, Ek!'
And crashing straight on
Is instantly gone.

## Moon-Horrors

When he has dined, the man-eating tiger leaves certain
    signs.
But nothing betrays the moon's hideous number nines.

Nobody knows where they sleep off their immense meals.
They strike so fatally nobody knows how one feels.
One-eyed, one-legged, they start out of the ground with
    such a shout
The chosen victim's eyes instantly fall out.
They do not leave so much as a hair but smack their chops
And go off thinner than ever with grotesque hops.

Now the shark will take a snack by shearing off half a
    swimmer.
Over the moon presides a predator even grimmer.
Descending without warning from the interstellar heavens
Whirling like lathes, arrive the fearful horde of number
    sevens.

Whatever they touch, whether owl or elephant, poet or
    scientist,
The wretched victim wilts instantly to a puff of purple mist
And before he can utter a cry or say goodbye to kith and
    kin
Those thin-gut number sevens have sucked him ravenously
    in.

Mosquitoes seem dreadful, for they drink at a man as he
    sleeps.
Night and day over the moon a far craftier horror creeps.
It is hard to know what species of creature you would have
    to be
To escape the attentions of the moon's horrible number
    three.
He attacks as a nightmare, and the sleeper dreams he is
    being turned inside out
And sucked dry like an orange, and when he wakes it has
    all come about.
Ever afterwards he is perfectly hollow and dry, while his
    precious insides

Nourish some gross number three wherever that monster
    now resides.

But the thing that specializes in hunting down the great
    hero
Is the flying strangler, the silent zero.

It is luckily quite rare, perhaps there is only one.
According to legend it lives sleepily coiled around the sun.
But when a moon-hero appears it descends and hovers just
   over his head.
His enemies call it a halo, but his friends see it and tremble
   with dread.
And sure enough, in the very best of his days,
That zero drops around his neck, tightens, and whirls
   away with him into the sun's blaze.

## Moon-Wind

There is no wind on the moon at all
   Yet things get blown about.
In utter utter stillness
   Your candle shivers out.

In utter utter stillness
   A giant marquee
Booms and flounders past you
   Like a swan at sea.

In utter utter stillness
   While you stand in the street
A squall of hens and cabbages
   Knocks you off your feet.

In utter utter stillness
   While you stand agog
A tearing twisting sheet of pond
   Clouts you with a frog.

A camp of caravans suddenly
   Squawks and takes off.
A ferris wheel bounds along the skyline
   Like a somersaulting giraffe.

Roots and foundations, nails and screws,
   Nothing holds fast,
Nothing can resist the moon's
   Dead-still blast.

79

## Moon-Tulips

Tulips on the moon are a kind of military band.
A bed of crimson ones will march up to your window and
     take its stand.
Then out of their flashing brass and silver they rip some
     Prussian fanfare.
Nobody asked them, and nobody takes any notice of their
     blare.
After a while, they about turn and to kettledrums
     goose-step away.
Soon under somebody else's window they are presenting
     the same deafening bouquet.


## Moon-Nasturtiums

Nasturtiums on earth are small and seething with horrible
     green caterpillars.
On the moon they are giant, jungles of them, and
     swarming with noisy gorillas.
And the green caterpillars there are the size of anacondas.
The butterflies that hatch from those are one of the moon's
     greatest wonders.
Though few survive the depredations of the gorillas
Who are partial to the succulent huge eggs that produce
     such caterpillars.


## Moon-Dog-Daisies

Dog-daisies on the moon run in packs
And it is their habit to carry moon-bees on their backs.
Dog-daisies live mainly on the small squealing sounders of
     sow-thistles
That charge about the moon's canyons, and the daisies are
     not deterred by their bristles.

When a sow-thistle has given up the ghost to the daisy-dogs
Those moon-bees pounce down on to the feast and make
   themselves hogs.

## Moon-Roses

The moon's roses are very odd,
Each one the size of a turkey.
Over the fields they ponderously plod
Since their flight is dangerously jerky.

They lay eggs
With one long ear and three rabbity legs
And hatch them by pulling their spigots out like kegs.

## Moon-Hops

Hops are a menace on the moon, a nuisance crop.
From hilltop to hilltop they hop hopelessly without stop.
Nobody knows what they want to find, they just go on till
   they drop,
Clip-clop at first, then flip-flop, then slip-slop, till finally
   they droopily drop and all their pods pop.

## Moon-Heads

Shining like lamps and light as balloons
Bodiless heads drift and bump among the moon's

Volcanoes, each like a demon-ghost,
A paper Chinese lantern kite that has got lost –

Except they are not made of paper O no,
They are made of astral light colder than any snow

And they are not ghosts – they never lived at all.
They are the spirit-shapes of unborn prehistoric monsters
   still awaiting the Creator's call,

Still waiting to be properly born and given bodies of flesh.
To walk about and eat and sleep and be normal is their
  only wish.

But they fear they are too late,
They fear they are out of date,

And they are probably right,
Therefore they gnash their fangs and shriek in the face of
  the lonely wayfarer at dead of night.


## Music on the Moon

The pianos on the moon are so long
The pianist's hand must be fifteen fingers strong.

The violins on the moon are so violent
They have to be sunk in deep wells, and then they only
  seem to be silent.

The bassoons on the moon blow no notes
But huge blue loons that flap slowly away with undulating
  throats.

Now harmonicas on the moon are humorous,
The tunes produce German Measles, but the speckles more
  numerous.

Of a trumpet on the moon you can never hear enough
Because it puffs the trumpeter up like a balloon and he
  floats off.

Double basses on the moon are a risk all right,
At the first note enormous black hands appear and carry
  away everything in sight.

Even a triangle on the moon is risky,
One ping – and there's your head a half bottle of Irish
  whisky.

In the same way, be careful with the flute –
Because wherever he is, your father will find himself
  converted into a disgusting old boot.

On the whole it's best to stick to the moon's drums.
Whatever damage they do is so far off in space the news
    never comes.

## Moon-Ways

The moon's roads are treacherous.
It is no good taking a bus.
The road that takes you home loyally
Year after year, suddenly cruelly
Runs you to jail instead.
Too late to shake your head
When the cell-door clangs shut.
Home is where you're put.

A road that had always led to your friends
One day abruptly ends
In a ghost-town –
Ceilings coming down,
Brambles in hallways, owls' nests in beds,
Mouldy playing cards, dolls' heads.

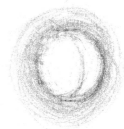

Some roads, more active, stray
Somewhere fresh every day –
Even from minute to minute.
A village so close that you are all but in it
Suddenly it's a lake –

You feel the road ripple like a snake
As it changes its mind.

Better leave roads behind.
Better just train your nose
And go as a bee goes.

## The Snail of the Moon

Saddest of all things on the moon is the snail without a shell.
You locate him by his wail, a wail heart-rending and terrible

Which sounds as though something had punctured him.
His battle for progress is both slow and grim.

He is sad, wet and cold, like a huge tear
In a thin skin. He wanders far and near

Searching for a shelter from the sun –
For the first sun-beam will melt and make him run.

So moving in moon-dark only he must keep going,
With muscles rippling and saliva flowing,

But nowhere on the moon is there garage
For such a snail. He is not merely large

He is over a mile from side to side.
It's useless him seeking any place to hide.

So wailingly and craning his periscopes
Over the dark bulge of the moon he gropes.

He has searched every inch of the moon. I guess
That silver is snail-saliva silveriness.


## Crab-Grass

When you get to the moon, watch out for crab-grass.
It is in complete control of the moon's badlands, alas.

It drives the foolish gooseberries in fat gaggling flocks
Over high cliffs so that they split and lie helplessly edible
    below on the rocks.

It herds the moon-potatoes through their great seas of
    volcanic ash
And nips their flippers so they leap ashore and flounder
    where they cannot so much as splash.

When a crab-grass comes upon a benighted tourist,
Of five hundred possible ends he may meet, that is the
    surest.

A crab-grass is ginger and hairy, and usually moves about
    six inches per year
In hordes of up to ten million, but that is its bottom gear.

You know a crab-grass is about to attack, by its excited hoot.
It has no eyes, so do not wait to see the whites of those
    before you shoot.


## Moon-Witches

The moon is a dusty place
But it's no good trying to sweep the dust up.
All the witches burned at the stake on earth
In the wicked times when that was a sport,
All those witches who worshipped the moon
Sent their scorched souls there to cool off.
So there they all are, living in the crannies
And looking exactly like cockroaches.
To all appearances they are in fact cockroaches,
Except they have a passion for brooms.
They forget what it is about brooms
So important to witches,
But they remember they are very important.
Seeing a broom, they become frantic,
They salivate, their tiny eyes swivel on stalks,
But all cockroaches can do is eat,
So they rush passionately at the broom
And passionately they devour it
Right down to the stick.

Then they zig-zag away frustrated,
Reminded of something important they cannot remember,
Splinters in their teeth and their eyes full of dust.


## The Moon-Hyena

The moon-hyena's laughter
Emerges at midnight or soon after

From a volcano's holes.
Its echo tumbles and rolls.
It grows like a moon quake, always louder, never softer,
    horrible laughter,

A laughter of dark hell,
Mad laughter of a skull,
Coming to devour the living ones.
You are wakened by the scare in your bones.
The moon-hyena is abroad, it is coming over the hill.

And it seems to you as you waken
The whole moon is being shaken
By its own ghastly amusement –
A crazy, cruel laughter, spreading amazement.

But then, just in time, you recall
The moon-hyena is not dangerous at all.
In spite of its moon-size terrific voice
It is about the size of a mouse
With a furry powder-puff tail.

And nobody is more distressed
By the laughter that erupts from its chest
Instead of sweet song, when it tries to sing,
Than this tiny creature, creeping along –

Yet it is so full of love and joy that sing it must, or bust.


## Mushrooms on the Moon

Mushrooms on the moon are delicious.
But those who eat them become birds, beasts, or fishes.
Space-fishes, space-beasts, and space-birds.
They stray out into space in shoals and flocks and herds.

At first, rapturous and excited,
But suddenly feeling space all round them and above and
    below they are affrighted.

Then goggling space-fish go fleeting in formations,
Space-beasts go trailing here and there in endless migrations,

Space-birds go hurtling from one end of space to the other
   in endless agitations
Among the constellations.

But space is too vast, they are lost, as if quite blind.
They are looking for the human bodies they left behind

On the tiny tiny moon, so tiny, tiny as a dust-grain

Which they can never hope to alight on again.


## The Adaptable Mountain Dugong

The Mountain Dugong is a simply fantastic animal.
It lives mainly in extinct volcanoes, uttering its lonely call
Which nobody answers, because it is the sole Mountain
   Dugong, there are no others at all.

It keeps alive with a number of surprising tricks.
It looks like a table, just as stick insects look like sticks.
So nobody interferes, they think it's an old table dumped
   there by passing hicks.

But lo, what is under that most common-looking table?
Spare heads and legs in great assortment, all looking very
   much alive and able.
The Mountain Dugong is its own Noah's Ark, and he will
   not be stuck with any one label.

For instance, here comes a pack of wild dogs, each with a
   mouth like a refuse bin.
They have smelt the Mountain Dugong's peculiar fried fish
   smell and want to get their teeth in,
Because wild dogs need to devour every living thing in all
   directions and to them this is no sin.

But the Mountain Dugong is already prepared, the wild
   dogs cannot shock it.
He unscrews his table-legs and screws a greyhound leg into
   each socket
And is off over the crater-edge with all his equipment in
   three leaps like a rubber rocket.

The wild dogs begin to wear him down, they head him in a
  circle, they bring him to a stop, they gather in a ring,
But all this time the Mountain Dugong has not been
  malingering.
He has screwed on to himself the headpiece of a tiger and
  in no time those wild dogs are a pile of chewed string.

This is how the adaptable Mountain Dugong carries on
  without loss.
He will screw on reindeer feet and head where there is
  nothing but Arctic moss.
Where there is nothing but sand the legs and hump of a
  camel soon get him across.

And he is forced to such tricks because there will never be
  another of his sort.
He has to keep himself in circulation by means no sane
  traveller would report.
I record his habits here, in case he should never again be
  seen or caught.


## Moon-Cloud Gripe

Moon-cloud gripe first shows
By a whitening of the nose.
Then your hair begins to stir,
Your eyes begin to blur.
Then you go blue,
You shiver and say 'Flu.'
Then between your fingertips
A blue spark skips.
Then an amazing red
Zag zigs up from your head
And splits the ceiling.
You have the feeling
You are going to explode.
You are rumbling like a road
Under a ten-ton wagon.
Then a long orange dragon

Like a rip-saw tears
From your mouth and flares
The furniture to ash.
Down you crash.
The walls split and shake.
Neighbours shout 'Earthquake!'
(How can they tell
It's just that you're not well?)

The only cure, they say,
Is to sigh for a whole day.


## Tree-Disease

On the moon with great ease
You can catch tree-disease.
The symptoms are birds
Seeming interested in your words
And examining your ears.
Then a root peers
From under the nail
Of your big toe, then
You'd better get cured quick
Or you'll be really sick.


## Cactus-Sickness

I hope you never contract
The lunar galloping cact-
us, which is when dimples
Suddenly turn to pimples,
And these pimples bud –
Except for the odd dud –
Each one into a head with hair
And a face just like the one you wear.
These heads grow pea-size to begin
From your brows, your nose, your cheeks and your chin.

But soon enough they're melon-size,
All with mouths and shining eyes.
Within five days your poor neck spreads
A bunch of ten or fifteen heads
All hungry, arguing or singing
(Somewhere under your own head's ringing).
And so for one whole tedious week
You must admit you are a freak.

And then, perhaps when you gently cough
For silence, one of the heads drops off.
Their uproar instantly comes to a stop.
Then in silence, plop by plop,
With eyes and mouth most firmly closed,
Your rival heads, in turn deposed,
Land like pumpkins round your feet.
You walk on feeling light and neat.

In the next mirror are assured
That now you stand completely cured.


## Moon-Weapons

There are weapons on the moon
Which behave oddly.
They appear, lying handy,
Near the ungodly.

The ungodly, he loves all weapons,
And when he meets one such
He just can't resist it.
He has to touch.

If it's a sword,
He strokes its moony blade,
And his eyes close with pleasure.
But it is moon-made.

And the next thing
The sword's evil spirit

Stares from that man's eyes
Red as a ferret.

And he is moon-mad
Till he stabs somebody –
Then moonier and madder
He laughs all bloody.

Then the sword chuckles and flees
On a hellish blast –
Leaving one dead man
And one man aghast.


## Moon-Cabbage

Cabbages on the moon are not cabbages.
They are little old women, gabbing old baggages.

Where our cabbages are bundles of leaves, gently
    flip-flapping,
Those are bundles of great loose lips, yappity-yap-yapping.

Yappity-yap, yappity-yap, yappity-yap-yap-yap!
Where our cabbages have hearts, those have gossip gushing
    out of a gap.

Not all of them are just bundles of lips. It appears
Some are in fact bundles of flapping ears, just like bundles
    of small elephant ears.

Flappity-flap, flappity-flap, flappity-flap-flap-flap!
Our cabbages are worn out by caterpillars, but those get
    ragged on sheer yap.

So some are all yap and some are all ears and their mutual
    amusements resound.
And they are so tough they can go on at that till their one
    scaly old shank grows right down into the ground.

## Moony Art

Whatever you want on the moon
You just draw a line round its outline
And it lumps into life – there it is.
If it's a dog it barks and needs feeding.
If it's a person – it's a person
And you'll have to look after him
Till he's learned to talk and manage.

You will see, you'll have to be careful
What you draw and how you draw it.
Most important, if you can't draw perfect
Better not draw. What you draw, you get.

If you draw a kneeless dog – you get one.
When he falls, you'll have to stand him up.
He has to sleep standing or leaning.
His whole life is an awful problem to him.

If you draw a hideous face – look out!
It will be your permanent attendant.
Staring across the table, or over your shoulder.
If you draw a snake – draw it fangless.
If you draw a tiger, first draw the cage.

So if you draw, draw only beautiful things,
Or pleasant happy things, or useful things.
And make sure you draw them perfect.
Outer space is one horrendous dump
Of people's careless doodles – dangerous and dreadful.
Better not draw at all than add to that.


## Moon-Thorns

The Moon's thorns
Are corkscrew curved horns
Waiting in a bush
To make a startling rush

And stab you to the bone.
While you groan
A drop of your blood
Soaks in where you stood.

From that tiny mote of moon-mud
Pokes a tiny bud.
It strengthens, it grows,
It opens a surprising face
And that is the moon-rose
Famed throughout space.

The horned bloom given
At marriages in heaven.

## Moon-Ravens

Are silver white
Like the moonlight
And their croak, their bark
Is not dark
And ominous,
But luminous
And a sweet chime
Always announcing time
For good news to come
If there is some,
And if there isn't
Then there's a moon-present –
That is, a stillness,
And if you have any illness
It flits out of your mouth
In the shape of a black moth

Which the moon-raven then follows
And swallows.

## Moon-Marriage

Marriage on the moon is rather strange.
It's nothing you can arrange.

You dream a frog comes in shivering from the moon-snow
And clings to you crying: 'O!O!O!
I am so happy you married me!'
You wake up frozen blue, and need a stiff brandy –
Lucky you, if you have one handy.

Or maybe a smiling wolf comes up close
While you doze off, in your chair, and gives you a kiss,
A cold wet doggy kiss, and then you know
You have been CHOSEN, and it's no good flailing awake
   bawling, 'No!'
Wherever the wolf is, she just goes on smiling –
It's an eerie feeling.

Or maybe deep in your sleep a mountain looms
With rumbling and lightning and misty glooms,
Whispering, 'Do you love me
As much as I love you?' And you wake
With your nose bleeding, and all one terrible ache
Like a worn-out mountaineer,
And still feeling the precipices near.

But there's no telling what bride
May choose you from the inside.
And if you're a girl you're no better off.
Before somebody normal can make you his wife
A Siberian tiger snatches you up in your sleep
And carries you to his cave under the glacier.
Then when you wake, while you dress and comb your hair,
And even long after, when you go out shopping,
You have only to close your eyes and you hear
Your tiger breathing near.
Woe betide any man then who enters your house.
He will be removed by your abnormal spouse.

If you're lucky you might be picked by a little bird, such as
   a swallow,
An undemanding fellow,
Who clears off six months in the year on a world hike
Leaving you to do as you like.

On the moon it is all a matter of luck
Is marriage.

And the only offspring are poems.


## The Moon-Mourner

The moon is haunted by a crying
Sobbing crying groaning crying

Person that you cannot see –
He cries, cries heartrendingly

Night or day no difference,
The wailing gibberish makes no sense,

Crying sadder than ever you heard
As if the end of the world had occurred

And now the news has reached the moon.
As it approaches you almost swoon,

As it comes close you almost drop.
On and on without a stop

And louder and louder and closer until
You think the fright of it might kill.

And now you think it has come for you.
There is nothing you can do.

And it is right inside you now.
But then it's passed, you don't know how.

You were a puddle it had to wade.
And slowly away you hear it fade

Among the craters white as snow
With its petrifying woe.


## The Dracula Vine

People on the moon love a pet.
But there's only one pet you can get –
The Dracula Vine, a monstrous sight!
But the moon-people like it all right.

This pet looks like a climbing plant
Made from parts of elephant.
But each flower is a hippo's head
Endlessly gaping to be fed.

Now this pet eats everything –
Whatever you can shovel or fling.
It snaps up all your old cardboard boxes
Your empty cans and your stuffed foxes.

And wonder of wonders! The very flower
You have given something to devour
Sprouts on the spot a luscious kind of pear
Without pips, and you can eat it there.

So this is a useful pet
And loyal if well-treat.
But if you treat it badly
It will wander off sadly

Till somebody with more garbage than you
Gives its flowers something to do.


## The Armies of the Moon

Many as the troubles upon the old moon are,
The worst is its unending Civil War.

The soldiers of the Moon-Dark are round and small.
Each clanks like a tank, blue armour covering all.

He wears asbestos overalls under his clatter.
So if he's thrown to the volcanoes it does not matter.
His weapon is a sackful of bloodsucking vampires
(Wars on the moon are without rules or umpires).
He flings these bats one at a time into the enemy host.
When it returns full he sends it to the first aid post
Where it gives up the blood for transfusions later in the
    battle.
Then it flies back to its owner with renewed mettle.

The soldiers of the Moon-Light are tall and thin.
They seem to be glisteningly naked, but are in fact silvered
    with tin.
They are defensive fighters, but pretty hot –
Their armament is an electric torch and a lobsterpot.
They flash their beam into the vampire's eyes and so
    puzzle it.
Then cram the lobsterpot on to its head, and so muzzle it.
They long for the last great battle in which they will catch
Every vampire the Moon-Darkers have been able to hatch.
Then they will rush upon the helpless Moon-Darkers and
    soon
With knitting-needles abolish them forever from the face of
    the moon.

## The Silent Eye

On the moon lives an eye.
It flies about in the sky,
Staring, glaring, or just peering.
You can't see what it uses for steering.
It is about the size of a large owl,
But has no feathers, and so is by no means a fowl.
Sometimes it zips overhead from horizon to horizon,
Then you know it has seen something surprisin'.
Mostly it hovers just above you and stares
Rudely down into your most private affairs.
Nobody minds it much, they say it has charm.

It has no mouth or hands, so how could it do harm?
Besides, as I say, it has these appealing ways.
When you are sitting sadly under crushing dismays,
This eye floats up and gazes at you like a mourner,
Then droops and wilts and a huge tear sags from its corner,
And soon it is sobbing and expressing such woe
You begin to wish it would stop it and just go.


## A Moon-Witch

A moon-witch is no joke.
She comes as a sort of smoke.
She whisps in through the keyhole and feels about
Like a spider's arm or a smoke-elephant's snout
Till she finds her victim.
He collapses like a balloon – she has sucked him
Empty in a flash. Her misty feeler
Blooms red as blood in water, then milkily paler –
And fades. And a hundred miles off
She disguises her burp with a laugh.

Also she has a sort of electronic
Rocket-homing trick – and that is chronic.
She steals the signature
Of whoever she wants to bewitch
And swallows it. Now wherever he might be
He sees her face, horrible with evil glee,
Hurtling at him like a rocket – WHOP!
People see him stop.
He staggers, he smooths his brow, he is astonished –
Whatever it was, it seems to have vanished.

He doesn't know what he's in for.
He's done for.

Only deep in sleep he dreams and groans
A pack of hyenas are fighting over his bones.

In a week, he dies. Then 'Goodness!' the witch says,
And yawns and falls asleep for about ten days –

Like a huge serpent that just ate
Something its own weight.


## The Moon-Mare

The moon-mare runs
On human mountains.

Wild as a ghost
She is here, she is past,

In her lunatic fury.
The only sure lure is

The music stolen
From stars that have fallen.

Play this to the twilight
In a silence. She may hear it.

She moves like nightfall.
Beautiful, beautiful.

Her horizons lose her.
And your hair freezes,

And in the chill dew
She is watching you.

When the music ends
There she stands.

What is she like?
You dare not look.

You sit in her stare.
You dare not stir.


## Foxgloves

Foxgloves on the moon keep to dark caves.
They come out at the dark of the moon only and in waves

Swarm through the moon-towns and wherever there's a
  chink
Slip into the houses and spill all the money, clink-clink,
And crumple the notes and rearrange the silver dishes,
And dip hands into the goldfish bowls and stir the
  goldfishes,
And thumb the edges of mirrors, and touch the sleepers
Then at once vanish into the far distance with a wild
  laugh leaving the house smelling faintly of Virginia
  creepers.

## A Moon Man-Hunt

A man-hunt on the moon is full of horrible sights and
  sounds.
There are these foxes in red jackets, they are their own
  horses and hounds.
They have unhuman eyes, O they are savage out of all
  bounds.

They swagger at the meet, their grins going back under
  their ears.
They are sociable to begin with, showing each other their
  long fangs and their no fears.
They pretend it is all a good game and nothing to do with
  death and its introductory tears.

Now one yip! and they are off, tails waving in sinister
  accord.
To tell the truth, they are a murderous depraved-looking
  horde.
Sniff sniff! they come over the acres, till some strolling
  squire looks up and sees them pattering toward.

The sweat jumps on his brow freezingly and the hair
  stands on his thighs.
His lips writhe, his tongue fluffs dry as a duster, tears pour
  from his eyes.

His bowels twist like a strong snake, and for some seconds
   he sways there useless with terrified surprise.
'Ha Ha!' go all the foxes in unison.
'That menace, that noble rural vermin, the gentry, there's
   one!'
The dirt flies from their paws and the squire begins
   hopelessly to run.

But what chance does that wretch have against such an
   animal?
Five catch his heels, and one on his nose, and ten on each
   arm, he goes down with a yell.
It is terrible, it is terrible, O it is terrible!


## Moon Transport

Some people on the moon are so idle
They will not so much as saunter, much less sidle.

But if they cannot bear to walk, or try,
How do they get to the places where they lie?

They gather together, as people do for a bus.
'All aboard, whoever's coming with us.'

Then they climb on to each other till they are all
Clinging in one enormous human ball.

Then they roll, and so, without lifting their feet,
Progress quite successfully down the street.


## Moon-Freaks

The half-man is a frequent freak,
   One ear, one eye, and so on.
He cannot turn the other cheek
   And has only one foot to go slow on.
      He can't ride a bicycle or hobby-horse.
      He does everything singlehanded of course.

Another sort of people look like a sort of pale spider.
They are actually nothing but huge human hands.
They gallop round on four fingers and the thumb sits up as
    a rider.

Another sort of people are condemned to being just feet,
Wandering about without ankles or knees or thighs.
They can't shake hands so they just kick when they meet.
They are great runners but since they have no eyes
Are constantly tripping on stones and charging into walls,
But they are so low they never get hurt in their falls.
A strange thing – if one stops, all the rest line up behind in
    a queue.
Otherwise they are quite useless and have nothing to do.

The moon's book-people simply love to read.
When they feel like reading, all they need
Is to meet with a friend. And thereupon
Each holds the other open and reads on.


## Moon-Clock

Glancing at the moon-clock
Always brings a weird shock.

Somehow, somehow
It is never now.

The time is Grizzly Bear
(No time to clean your nails or do your hair)

Or the time is Oak
(Nobody's time to speak, nobody spoke)

Or the time is Rain
(Soon you'll be born and visit your grave again)

Or the time is River
(Am I here all the time or gone forever?)

Or the time is Shooting Star
(Too late to try again, stay where you are)

Or the time is still to come
And the clock's hands are stopped and the tock is dumb.


## Moon-Walkers

After a bad night's sleeping
All night the full moon's glare seeping
Between your closed eyelids, and you tossing and turning
With dreams of heaven burning
And cellars smoking with mystery
And erupting and debouching monsters from prehistory,

You wake with a cracking headache and eyes
Like lumps of lead, and to your intense surprise
You see all over the ceiling giant foot-tracks
Which have nothing to do with the blotches and cracks.

Enormous foot-prints of the lizard sort
Give you gooseflesh and sink you deep in thought.

So you carefully get out of bed
Ready to see your foot enclosed in an alligator-type head,

But your house is quite empty, not even a newt in a cup,
Only these giant mud-splodge claw-foot prints all over the
    ceilings wherever you look up

And all over the walls and everywhere
Over the furniture and the linen and then your hair

Really stands on end as you realise every one
Of these tramplers must have weighed at least a ton,

Nevertheless they came out like the far stars noiseless and
    weightless in the night
And vanished at first light

As if it were only the light which keeps them hid –
Or as if they came out of your dreams and went back in
    there (which they probably did).

# Moon-Bells

The savage tribes that have their lairs
   In the moon's extinct craters
Pray to the earth with savage prayers:
   'O Thou who didst create us

Speak to us through our Holy bells.
   O with thy wisdom guide us.
Correct with bong of decibels
   The lunatic inside us.'

So then they swing the bells they have slung
   In each volcano's womb,
And Earth begins to declare with clung
   And clang and mumbling boom

Out of one bell: 'Towers fall
   And dunghills rise.' And from another:
'He who thinks he knows it all
   Marries his own mother.'

'Only an owl knows the worth of an owl,'
   Clanks one with a clunk.
'Let every man,' groans one in toil,
   'Skin his own skunk.'

'The head is older than the book,'
   Shrills one with sour tone,
And 'Beauty is only skin deep,
   But ugly goes to the bone.'

Then: 'He who does not swell in the warm
   Will not shrink in the cold.'
Another is muttering: 'Hair by hair
   You may pluck a tiger bald.'

'Going to ruin is silent work,'
   One dins with numbing bellow.
And: 'Love and Thirst, they know no shame,
   But the Itch beats them hollow.'

'All things, save Love and Music,
　　Shall perish,' another cries.
'Downcast is King of illness.'
　　'Dead fathers have huge eyes.'

So on and on the bells declare
The Word of Earth to them up there.


## A Moon-Hare

So I run out. I am holding a hare.
With a million terrified people I stare

From the point of Manhattan, across the Atlantic.
The skies are in flames. The people are frantic.

The moon is hurtling hugely toward
The crouching earth and its cringing horde.

Huger, and golder, and growing to shatter
Our globe of skyscrapers and water.

And I see, as it bulges and overhangs,
It is teeming with fiery, terrible things.

And I see, as it looms, it is packed to burst
With insect, fish, and bird and beast,

And the trees and the blossoms of Paradise,
And each is a miracle Paradise

Crammed with miracles. I watch it grow.
I hear earth's people screaming 'No!'

As it rolls under the glistening horizon.
Then comes the world-ending collision

Flinging us flat. That impact jars
Us into a space with different stars.

The skyscrapers, blazed-out with the shock,
Frail as spider-web curtains they rock.

The big-eyed, up-eared hare I hold
Is solid flame of living gold.


## Singing on the Moon

Singing on the moon seems precarious.
Hum the slightest air
And some moon-monster sails up and perches to stare.
These monsters are moonily various.

If you sing in your bath
Risks are one of these monster entities
Will come crash through the wall and with dusty eyes
Perch on the taps to stare, as if in wrath.

The tenor who practises on a volcano side
Sees eyes rising over the crater rim
To fix their incredulity on him –
There is no place on the moon where a singer can hide

And not raise some such being face to face.
But do not be alarmed – their seeming fury
Comes from their passion for music being so fiery.
So if you just sing from your heart, and stay in your place,

At your song's end the monster will cry out madly
And fling down money, probably far more than you can
    spend,
And kiss your shoe with his horrific front-end,
Then shudder away with cries of rapture diminishing sadly.


## The Moon-Bull

Beautiful O beautiful
Is the moon-bull.
Mild, immense and white
He sniffs the moist night.

He sniffs the black hole
Through which slowly roll

The teeming galaxies.
He is always at ease.

He thinks Night is his cow.
There he stands now
Licking the glossy side
Of his infinite bride.


## Earth-Moon

Once upon a time there was a person
He was walking along
He met the full burning moon
Rolling slowly toward him
Crushing the stones and houses by the wayside.
He shut his eyes from the glare.
He drew his dagger
And stabbed and stabbed and stabbed.
The cry that quit the moon's wounds
Circled the earth.
The moon shrank, like a punctured airship,
Shrank, shrank, smaller, smaller,
Till it was nothing
But a silk handkerchief, torn,
And wet as with tears.
The person picked it up. He walked on
Into moonless night
Carrying this strange trophy.

# UNDER THE NORTH STAR

## Amulet

Inside the Wolf's fang, the mountain of heather.
Inside the mountain of heather, the Wolf's fur.
Inside the Wolf's fur, the ragged forest.
Inside the ragged forest, the Wolf's foot.
Inside the Wolf's foot, the stony horizon.
Inside the stony horizon, the Wolf's tongue.
Inside the Wolf's tongue, the Doe's tears.
Inside the Doe's tears, the frozen swamp.
Inside the frozen swamp, the Wolf's blood.
Inside the Wolf's blood, the snow wind.
Inside the snow wind, the Wolf's eye.
Inside the Wolf's eye, the North Star.
Inside the North Star, the Wolf's fang.

## The Loon

The Loon, the Loon
Hatched from the Moon

Writhes out of the lake
Like an airborne snake.

He swallows a trout
And then shakes out

A ghastly cry
As if the sky
Were trying to die.

## The Wolverine

The gleeful evil Wolverine
  Lopes along.
'O I am going to devour everybody and everything!'
  Is his song.

With gloating cackle the glutton gobbles
  The Eagle's brood.
Snaps the sleeping Snowy Owl's head off, chuckling
  'This is good!'

The trapped Wolf's pelt will not adorn
  The trapper's wall –
The Wolverine's swallowed it with a wild laugh
  Trap and all.

When he bobs up in the Northern Lights
  With more merry tales
The Bear feels the skull creak under his scalp
  And his smile fails.

The gleeful evil Wolverine
  Belly full of song
Sings: 'I am coming to swallow you all, hiya!'
  Loping along.


## The Snowy Owl

Yellow Eye O Yellow Eye
Yellow as the yellow Moon.

Out of the Black Hole of the North
The Ice Age is flying!

The Moon is flying low –
The Moon looms, hunting her Hare –

The Moon drops down, big with frost
And hungry as the end of the world.

The North Pole, rusty-throated,
Screeches, and the globe shudders –

The globe's eyes have squeezed shut with fear.
But the stars are shaking with joy.

And look!

The Hare has a dazzling monument!
A big-eyed blizzard standing

On feet of black iron!
Let us all rejoice in the Hare!

Snowy Owl O Snowy Owl
Staring the globe to stillness!

The Moon flies up.

A white mountain is flying.

The Hare has become an angel!


## The Black Bear

The Bear's black bulk
Is solid sulk.

He mopes with his nose
Between his toes

Or rears with a roar
Like a crashed-back door
Shouting: 'God swore

I'd be Adam –
And here I am

In Paradise!'
But then his eyes

Go pink with rage:
'But I am in a cage

Of rough black hair!
I have to wear

These dungfork hands!
And who understands

The words I shout
Through this fanged snout?

I am God's laugh!
I am God's clown!'

Then he glooms off
And lays him down

With a flea in his ear
To sleep till next year.

## An Evening Seal

Under fingers of blood
The islands dripped red
But the Clams in their bared bed
Gasped with blue cold.

And the Seal there, the Seal O
She raised her oiled head.
My fingers had died.
But the Seal's wake sliced open

A serpent of crestings –
Unscrolling a long gash
In ocean's ripe flesh

As robed in her silks
She plunged with her razors

Under cold of such steel
I was frightened to feel.

# The Muskellunge

An interplanetary torpedo
Fell into the lake long ago
When worlds were being made.

Now he searches the abyss
With the hunger of a sun of ice.

Muskellunge hid his soul, where it's safe.
In the middle of the earth.
Then took a job with the lake
As jaws
For the hunger of sunk bedrock.

When the Heavens fell, this old witchdoctor
Rescued all the gods in one bag
And swallowed it. He has them safe in his belly.
Now he eats only for them.

There he lies
Wiser than Orion and older than the Great Bear

Waiting for the ages to pass.


# A Lynx

The hushed limbs of forest,
Of clouds, of mountains, here
Take their hard-earned rest
Under the Lynx's ear.
In his sleep, they sleep –
As in a deep lake – deep.

Do not disturb this beast
Or clouds will open eyes,
Soundless the forest
Will fold away all its trees
And hazy the mountains
Fade among their stones.

# The Snow-Shoe Hare

The Snow-Shoe Hare
Is his own sudden blizzard.

Or he comes, limping after the snowstorm,
A big, lost, left-behind snowflake
Crippled with bandages.

White, he is looking for a great whiteness
To hide in
But the starry night is on his track –

His own dogged shadow
Panics him to right, and to left, and backwards,
    and forwards –
Till he skids skittering
Out over the blue ice, meeting the Moon.

He stretches, craning slender
Listening
For the Fox's icicles and the White Owl's slow cloud.

In his popping eyes
The whole crowded heaven struggles softly.

Glassy mountains, breathless, brittle forests
Are frosty aerials
Balanced in his ears.

And his nose bobs wilder
And his hot red heart thuds harder

Tethered so tightly
To his crouching shadow.


# Woodpecker

Woodpecker is rubber-necked
    But has a nose of steel.

He bangs his head against the wall
  And cannot even feel.

When Woodpecker's jack-hammer head
  Starts up its dreadful din
Knocking the dead bough double dead
  How do his eyes stay in?

Pity the poor dead oak that cries
  In terrors and in pains.
But pity more Woodpecker's eyes
  And bouncing rubber brains.

## The Musk-Ox

Express blizzards rumble, a horizontal snow-haulage,
Over the roof of the world.
The weathercock up there
Is the Musk-Ox, in his ankle-length hair.

Inside the skyslide steep continent of white darkness,
  under walloping wheels of wind,
He clings to his eyes –
A little castle with two windows
Like a fish on the bed of a flood river.

The stars are no company.
They huddle at the bottom of their aeons, only just
  existing,
Jostled by every gust,
Pinned precariously to their flutters of light,
Tense and weightless, ready to be snatched away into some
  other infinity.

And the broken tree-dwarves in their hollow, near him,
Have no energy for friendship, no words to spare,
Just hanging on, not daring to think of the sucking and
  bottomless emptiness of the blast
That grabs at their nape, and pounds their shoulders.

And the mountains stare towards them fadingly
Like solid-frozen mammoths staring at a Coca-Cola sign.

And the seas, heaping and freezing, neighbour him
    unknowingly
Like whales
Shouldering round a lost champagne cork.

He's happy.
Bowed beneath his snowed-under lean-to of horns,
Hunched over his nostrils, singing to himself,
Happy inside there, bent at his hearth-glow
Over the simple picture book
Of himself
As he was yesterday, as he will be tomorrow

While the Pole groans
And skies fall off the world's edge and the stars cling
    together.

## The Heron

The Sun's an iceberg
In the sky.
In solid freeze
The fishes lie.

Doomed is the Dab.
Death leans above –

But the Heron
Poised to stab
Has turned to iron
And cannot move.

## The Grizzly Bear

I see a bear
Growing out of a bulb in wet soil licks its black tip
With a pink tongue its little eyes
Open and see a present an enormous bulging mystery
    package
Over which it walks sniffing at seams

Digging at the wrapping overjoyed holding the joy off
  sniffing and scratching
Teasing itself with scrapings and lickings and the thought
  of it
And little sips of the ecstasy of it

O bear do not open your package
Sit on your backside and sunburn your belly
It is all there it has actually arrived
No matter how long you dawdle it cannot get away
Shamble about lazily laze there in the admiration of it
With all the insects it's attracted all going crazy
And those others the squirrel with its pop-eyed amazement
The deer with its pop-eyed incredulity
The weasel pop-eyed with envy and trickery
All going mad for a share wave them off laze
Yawn and grin let your heart thump happily
Warm your shining cheek fur in the morning sun

You have got it everything for nothing

## Brooktrout

The Brooktrout, superb as a matador,
Sways invisible there
In water empty as air.

The Brooktrout leaps, gorgeous as a jaguar,
But dropping back into swift glass
Resumes clear nothingness.

The numb-cold current's brain-wave is lightning –
No good shouting: 'Look!'
It vanished as it struck.

You can catch Brooktrout, a goggling gewgaw –
But never the flash God made
Drawing the river's blade.

# The Wendigo

The Wendigo's tread
Is a ghostly weight
On top of the head.

His footprints go deep
Through the nightmare drifts
Of the trapper's sleep

The Wendigo creaks
From trap to trap
And releasing the shrieks

The trapped corpse felt
He drinks up its soul
Leaving only the pelt

So the Wendigo swells
With a storm of souls
And their dying yells.

On a snow lake, soon,
The trapper shall stare
At the sudden Moon

And know his life's done
As the Wendigo sweeps
Through his skeleton

Like an owl of wind
With the blizzard wraiths
Of the creatures he skinned

Snatching his soul
To the shuddering lights
That fly with the Pole.

## The Osprey

The fierce Osprey
Prays over the bay.

God hides below
In his shadow.

Let God reveal
His scaly, cold
And shining brow –

Osprey shall fold
His wings and bow
His head and kneel.

## Mooses

The goofy Moose, the walking house-frame,
Is lost
In the forest. He bumps, he blunders, he stands.

With massy bony thoughts sticking out near his ears –
Reaching out palm upwards, to catch whatever might be
    falling from heaven –
He tries to think,
Leaning their huge weight
On the lectern of his front legs.

He can't find the world!
Where did it go? What does a world look like?
The Moose
Crashes on, and crashes into a lake, and stares at the
    mountain, and cries
'Where do I belong? This is no place!'

He turns and drags half the lake out after him
And charges the cackling underbrush –

He meets another Moose.
He stares, he thinks 'It's only a mirror!'

'Where is the world?' he groans, 'O my lost world!
And why am I so ugly?
And why am I so far away from my feet?'

He weeps.
Hopeless drops drip from his droopy lips.

The other Moose just stands there doing the same.

Two dopes of the deep woods.


## The Arctic Fox

No feet. Snow.
Ear – a star-cut
Crystal of silence.
The world hangs watched.

Jaws flimsy as ice
Champ at the hoar-frost
Of something tasteless –
A snowflake of feathers.

The forest sighs.
A fur of breath
Empty as moonlight
Has a blue shadow.

A dream twitches
The sleeping face
Of the snow-lit land.

When day wakes
Sun will not find
What night hardly noticed.


## Puma

God put the Cougar on the Mountain
To be the organist
Of the cathedral-shaped echoes.

Her screams play the hollow cliffs, the brinks
And the abyss.
Her music amazes the acoustics.

She lifts the icy shivering summit
Of her screech
And climbs it, looking for her Maker.

A crazy-gaze priestess of caverns –
All night she tries to break into heaven
With a song like a missile, while the Moon frosts her face.

All day afterwards, worn out,
She sleeps in the sun.

Sometimes – half-melted
In the sheet-flame silence –
Opens one jewel.


## Skunk

Skunk's footfall plods padded
    But like the thunder-crash
He makes the night woods nervous
    And wears the lightning-flash –

From nose to tail a zigzag spark
    As warning to us all
That thunderbolts are very like
    The strokes he can let fall.

That cloudburst soak, that dazzling bang
    Of stink he can let drop
Over you like a cloak of tar
    Will bring you to a stop.

O Skunk! O King of Stinkards!
    Only the Moon Knows
You are her prettiest, ugliest flower,
    Her blackest, whitest rose!

# Goose

The White Bear, with smoking mouth, embraces
All the North.
The Wild Goose listens.

South, south –
                 the Goose stretches his neck
Over the glacier.

And high, high
Turns the globe in his hands.

Hunts with his pack from star to star.
Sees the sun far down behind the world.

Sinks through fingers of light, with apricot breast,
To startle sleeping farms, at apple dawn,
With iceberg breath.

Then to and fro all Christmas, evening and morning,
Urging his linked team,
Clears the fowler's gun and the surf angler.

Homesick
Smells the first flower of the Northern Lights –

Clears the Lamb's cry, wrestles heaven,
Sets the globe turning.

Clears the dawns – a compass tolling
North, north.
                 North, north.

Wingbeat wading the flame of evening.

Till he dips his eyes
In the whale's music

Among the boom
Of calving glaciers

And wooing of wolves
And rumpus of walrus.

## Wolf

The Iron Wolf, the Iron Wolf

Stands on the world with jagged fur.
The rusty Moon rolls through the sky.
The iron river cannot stir.
The iron wind leaks out a cry

Caught in the barbed and iron wood.
The Iron Wolf runs over the snow
Looking for a speck of blood.
Only the Iron Wolf shall know

The iron of his fate.
He lifts his nose and moans,
Licks the world clean as a plate
And leaves his own bones.

## The Mosquito

To get into life
Mosquito died many deaths.

The slow millstone of Polar ice, turned by the Galaxy,
Only polished his egg.

Subzero, bulging all its mountain-power,
Failed to fracture his bubble.

The lake that held him swelled black,
Tightened to granite, with splintering teeth,
But only sharpened his needle.

Till the strain was too much, even for Earth.
Winter sank to her knees.

The stars drew off, trembling.
The mountains sat back, sweating.

The lake burst.

Mosquito

Flew up singing, over the broken waters –

A little haze of wings, a midget sun.


## Eagle

Big wings dawns dark.
The Sun is hunting.
Thunder collects, under granite eyebrows.

The horizons are ravenous.
The dark mountain has an electric eye.
The sun lowers its meat-hook.

His spread fingers measure a heaven, then a heaven.
His ancestors worship only him,
And his children's children cry to him alone.

His trapeze is a continent.
The Sun is looking for fuel
With the gaze of a guillotine.

And already the White Hare crouches at the sacrifice,
Already the Fawn stumbles to offer itself up
And the Wolf-Cub weeps to be chosen.

The huddle-shawled lightning-faced warrior
Stamps his shaggy-trousered dance
On an altar of blood.

# Tigress

She grin-lifts
Her black lips and white whiskers
As she yearns forward

Complaining
Tearing complaint off and banging it down a long pipe
That echoes and hums after

Her stride floats
Enjoying a weightlessness
A near-levitation

Again her cry
Scours out the drum of her
Her face

Works at its lacks and longings and quells
Its angers and rehearses its revenges
Endlessly

She lifts again
The welded and bolted plates of her head
Like an illness past curing

She rolls groaning
A bullet of anguish out of her

She is moving, in her hanging regalia
Everything in her is moving, slipping away forward
From the hindward-taper, drawing herself
Out of the air, like a tail out of water

A bow on the war-path, carrying itself
With its dazzling and painted arrows

Shoulders walling her chest, she goes
Between travelling armed walls

Lifting her brow as she walks to ripple
The surface of the element she moves in

Her cry rips the top off the air first
Then disembowels it

She lies down, as if she were lowering
A great snake into the ground

She rests her head on her forepaws, huge trouble
All her lines too enormous for her

I look into her almond eyes. She frowns
Them shut, the fur moving down on her brows.


## Tiger

At the junction of beauty and danger
The tiger's scroll becomes legible.
In relief, he moves through an impotent chaos.
The Creator is his nearest neighbour.
The mild, frosty, majestic mandala
Of his face, to spirit hospitable
As to flesh. With easy latitude
He composes his mass.
He exhales benediction,
Malediction. Privileged
At the paradoxical cross-junction
Of good and evil, and beyond both.
His own ego is unobtrusive
Among the jungle babblers,
His engineering faultlessly secure.
In a fate like an allegory
Of God-all-but-forgotten, he balances modestly
The bloodmarks of his canvas
And the long-grass dawn beauty
As the engraved moment of lightning
On the doomsday skin of the Universe.

# A Mountain Lion

A mountain lion, her alarmed skulk
Fearing to peel her molten umber
From shadows –
                    Her forefeet
Go forward daringly, a venture, a theft in them
Stealing her body away after –

She weaves, her banner's soft prisoner,
In her element of silence, weaving silence
Like a dance, a living silence
Making herself invisible magical steps
Weaving a silence into all her limbs

She flows along, just inside the air
Every line eluding the eye. Hesitation
And moving beyond
And by hesitation. All her legs like
A magical multiplication of one leg
Look at any one, the others are doing the walking
And slender and pressing
Forward through silence, becoming silence
Ahead and leaving it behind, travelling
Like a sound-wave, arriving suddenly.
Ahead of herself, a swift stillness.


# Live Skull

In the lake, behind the mirror

The Pike, a megalith.
Under the flame-flutter
Complexion of water.

The Pike, a sunk lintel
Balanced on stones
Under the crawling nape of light.

The Pike
Non-participant
Under the lake's slow lungs.

The Pike that has somehow, unmoving,
Sailed out of the sun

Into this measured hole –
Cold
A finger

Of the silence of space –
Slow
A smile

Of the deafness of earth

Making the skull creak.


## Off-Days

In the lowest pit of the solstice, among sour conifers,
The reservoir looked reluctant.
Shrunk low, lying as if ill
Beneath its rusty harness of old waterlines.
Its only life – shivers of patience.

Man-made and officially ugly
Its bed is a desert of black, private depression.
A second whole day we have called for a pike.
Nothing volunteers for election.

If there is one last pike – one old mule,
One last patriot,
It starves, resolutely legless,
Hunger closed,
Habit hardening to total absence
In this grave of spontaneity.

Wind off the lake-face, unexpected blows
Bleak as a knuckle
Is the water's only peevish trick.

Only try to imagine our dredging lures
Resurrecting one jerk of life
In the eyeballs
Of mud.

For days somebody's dead herring has lain
Miserably visible,
Like a failed bribe.

Finish!
The pike here
Have been reabsorbed by the outcrop.

All jaws have resumed the Jurassic!

*from* WHAT IS THE TRUTH?

from *What is the Truth?*

## Partridge

A grand bird is the Partridge, a wild weed of a sort.
The cheapest weed on all my ground, it never costs a
  thought.
And when it puffs and flies it's Bang! and Bang! and pretty
  sport.

I love to see them racing on their bumpy little wheels
And hear their rusty axles twisting out their creaks and
  squeals –
They're plumping up the sweetest, whitest meat of all my
  meals.

A son of the soil the Partridge is, from earth-clods he was
  born.
I love to see him crane his neck up, out of the young, green
  corn.
And better than bottled beer and skittles when the stubble's
  shorn

I love it when a covey Whoosh! explodes with such a rattle
And every bit spins whizzing and it's Bang! and Bang! a
  battle,
And dinner comes tumbling out of the air! Better than
  bedding cattle!

## Bess My Badger

Bess my badger grew up
In a petshop in Leicester. Moony mask
Behind mesh. Blear eyes
Baffled by people. Customers cuddled her,

Tickled her belly, tamed her – her wildness
Got no exercise. Her power-tools,
Her miniature grizzly-bear feet,
Feet like little garden-forks, had to be satisfied

Being just feet,
Trudging to-fro, to-fro, in her tight cage,
Her nose brushed by the mesh, this way, that way,
All night, every night, keeping pace

With the badgers out in the woods. She was
Learning to be a prisoner. She was perfecting
Being a prisoner. She was a prisoner. Till a girl
Bought her, to free her, and sold her to me.

What's the opposite of taming? I'm unteaching
Her tameness. First, I shut her in a stable.

But she liked being tame. That night, as every night,
At a bare patch of wall the length of her cage
To-fro, to-fro, she wore at the wood with her nose,
Practising her prison shuffle, her jail walk.

All day, dozing in the gloom, she waited for me.
Every supper-time, all she wanted was
Me to be a badger, and romp with her in the straw.
She laughed – a chuckling sort of snarl, a rattle,

And grabbed my toe in my shoe, and held it, hard,
Then rolled on to her back to be tickled.
'Be wild,' I told her. 'Be a proper badger.'
She twisted on to her feet, as if she agreed

And listened. Her head lifted – like a hand
Shaped to cast a snake's head shadow on the wall –
What she'd heard was a car. She waddled away
Shawled in her trailing cape of grey feathers,

And looked back. Sniffed a corner. Listened.

I could see she was lonely.
                                A few nights later
Her claws went wild. And they tunnelled
From stable to stable, connecting four stables.

Then bored up through the wall so the long loft
Became her look-out. After that,
If shouting in the yard, or a tractor, disturbed her,
You'd see her peering down through the dusty panes,

And if the loft door had been blown open
She'd poke her face out, furious, then slam it.
Soon she'd quarried out through the back of the stables
And with about three cartloads of stony rubble

From under the stables, she landscaped her porchway –
And the world was hers. Now, nightly,
Whatever she can shift, she'll shift, or topple,
For the worm, the beetle, or the woodlouse beneath it.

She tasted clematis roots, and now she's an addict.
She corkscrews holes in the wet lawn with her nose,
Nipping out the lobworms. With her mine-detector
Finds all the flower-bulbs. Early workmen meet her

Plodding, bowlegged, home through the village.

Already she hardly needs me. Will she forget me?
Sometimes I leave black-treacle sandwiches,
A treat at her entrance, just to remind her –
She's our houseproud lodger, deepening her rooms.

Or are we her lodgers? To her
Our farm-buildings are her wild jumble of caves,
Infested by big monkeys. And she puts up with us –
Big noisy monkeys, addicted to diesel and daylight.


Badger

The Badger in the spinney is the true king of this land.
All creatures are his tenants, though not all understand.

Didicoi red and roe-deer, gypsy foxes, romany otters –
They squabble about their boundaries, but all of them are
    squatters.

Even the grandest farm-house, what is it but a camp
In the land where the singing Badger walks the woods with
   his hooded lamp?

A farmer's but a blowing seed with a flower of crops and
   herds.
His tractors and his combines are as airy as his words.

But the Badger's fort was dug when the whole land was
   one oak.
His face is his ancient coat of arms, and he wears the same
   grey cloak

As if time had not passed at all, as if there were no such
   thing,
As if there were only the one night-kingdom and its Badger
   King.


## New Foal

Yesterday he was nowhere to be found
In the skies or under the skies.

Suddenly he's here – a warm heap
Of ashes and embers, fondled by small draughts.

A star dived from outer space – flared
And burned out in the straw.
Now something is stirring in the smoulder.
We call it a foal.

Still stunned
He has no idea where he is.
His eyes, dew-dusky, explore gloom walls and a glare
   doorspace.
Is this the world?
It puzzles him. It is a great numbness.

He pulls himself together, getting used to the weight of
   things
And to that tall horse nudging him, and to this straw.

He rests
From the first blank shock of light, the empty daze
Of the questions –
What has happened? What am I?

His ears keep on asking, gingerly.

But his legs are impatient,
Recovering from so long being nothing
They are restless with ideas, they start to try a few out,
Angling this way and that,
Feeling for leverage, learning fast –

And suddenly he's up

And stretching – a giant hand
Strokes him from nose to heel
Perfecting his outline, as he tightens
The knot of himself.
              Now he comes teetering
Over the weird earth. His nose
Downy and magnetic, draws him, incredulous,
Towards his mother. And the world is warm
And careful and gentle. Touch by touch
Everything fits him together.

Soon he'll be almost a horse.
He wants only to be Horse,
Pretending each day more and more Horse
Till he's perfect Horse. Then unearthly Horse
Will surge through him, weightless, a spinning of flame
Under sudden gusts,

It will coil his eyeball and his heel
In a single terror – like the awe
Between lightning and thunderclap.

And curve his neck, like a sea-monster emerging
Among foam,

And fling the new moons through his stormy banner,
And the full moons and the dark moons.

# Cow (I)

There's comfort in the Cow, my dear, she's mother to
  us all.
When Adam was a helpless babe, no mother heard
  him call.
The Moon saw him forsaken and she let a white star fall.

Beasts sharpened their noses when his cry came on the air.
Did a she-wolf nurse him with her wolf-cubs in the lair?
Or cuffed among rough bear-cubs was he suckled by a
  bear?

No, the gentle Cow came, with her queenly, stately tread,
Swinging her dripping udder, and she licked his face and
  head,
And ever since that moment on the Cow's love he has fed.

A man is but a bare baboon, with starlit frightened eyes.
As earth rolls into night he cheers himself with monkey
  cries
And wraps his head in dreams, but his lonely spirit flies

To sleep among the cattle in the warm breath of the herd.
Among the giant mothers, he lies without a word.
In timeless peace they chew their cud, till the first bird

Lifts the earth back into the clock, the spirit back into
  the man.
But the herd stays in Paradise, where everything began,
Where the rivers are rivers of foaming milk and the eyes
  are African.


# Cow (II)

The Cow is but a bagpipe,
All bag, all bones, all blort.
They bawl me out of bed at dawn
And never give a thought

a thought
They never give a thought.

The milk-herd is a factory:
Milk, meat, butter, cheese.
You think these come in rivers? O
The slurry comes in seas
                    seas
The slurry comes in seas.

A cowclap is an honest job,
A black meringue for the flies.
But when the sea of slurry spills
Your shining river dies
                    dies
Your shining river dies.

Say this about cows:
Nothing can stop
From one end the Moo
From t'other the flop
            flop
            flop
            flippety-flop
Floppety-flippety.

## Cow (III)

I think
There's a summer ocean liner in cows –
Majestic and far off,
With a quiet mysterious delight,
Fading through the blue afternoon.

And there's a ruined holy city
In a herd of lying down, cud-chewing cows –
Noses raised, eyes nearly closed
They are fragments of temples – even their outlines
Still at an angle unearthly.

As if a ray from heaven still rested across their brows,
As if they felt it, a last ray.

And now they come, swinging their ballast, bowing
As if they dragged slow loads slightly uphill,
There's a dance in the swaying walk of cows

With their long dancers' necks, to left and to right
And that slight outfling of hooves, a slow dance-step –
Bodies of oil,
Dancers coming from hard labour in the fields.

And there's a flare of wide skirts when they swirl
On such exact feet
With the ankles of tall dancers

In under the girders and asbestos.


## Shire Horses

One time we had nothing else of course and handsome
    they were.
We have a picture of our old horses, like a blurred pair
Of Victorian Grandads, in their beards and fobs, at a
    Country Fair.

You'd never believe the elastic in them, their nimbleness
    and their power.
Though they'd look like whispy old haystacks, propped-up
    and leaning there,
They could earth-quake like floodwater, brown-backed and
    tossing over a weir.

Every road and yard reeked of horses, they were
    everywhere.
Hard to credit it now. I sometimes dream I'm back there,
    my stare
Sunk in the wave that lifts and sprawls aside from the
    ploughshare.

It's like a dream of riding the boughs of a windy, working
    tree,

An oak that rips the live ground open, tearing its tap-root
    free.
My horses are great, creaking boughs. And all I seem to see

Is their huge, plum-tight haunches revolving, heavily, like
    mill-wheels.
Watery quake-weights. Wading the earth, like old shaggy
    angels.
I'd gaze into their furnace glow and go in a daze for miles.

Our last friendly angels – that's what they were.
Their toil was a kind of worship, their every step a bowing
    of prayer
Hidden under tangled hair and sweat. But the tractor
    shoved them all

Straight back to God. It didn't take much to undo them.
They were made of the stuff of souls, and the little grey
    Ferguson rattled straight through them.
Now you will not see them. But I saw them.


## Rat-Psalm

Sing the hole's plume, the rafter's cockade
Who melts from the eye-corner, the soft squealer
Pointed at both ends, who chews through lead

Sing the scholarly meek face
Of the penniless Rat
Who studies all night
To inherit the house

Sing the riffraff of the roof-space, who dance till dawn
Sluts in silk, sharpers with sleek moustaches
Dancing the cog-roll, the belly-bounce, the trundle

Sing the tireless hands
Of the hardworking Rat
Who demolishes the crust, and does not fail
To sign the spilt flour.

The Rat the Rat the Ratatatat
The house's poltergeist, shaped like a shuttle
Who longs to join the family

Sing his bright face, cross-eyed with eagerness
His pin fingers, that seem too small for the job
Sing his split nose, that looks so sore
O sing his fearless ears, the listener in the wall
Let him jump on your head, let him cling there
Save him from sticks and stones

Sing the Rat so poor he thrives on poison
Who has nothing to give to the trap, though it gapes for a
      year
Except his children
Who prays only to the ferret
'Forget me' and to the terrier
'In every million of me, spare two'

Who stuffs his velvet purse, in hurry and fear
With the memory of the fork,
The reflections of the spoons, the hope of the knives
Who woos his wife with caperings, who thinks deep

Who is the slave of two fangs

O sing
The long-tailed grey worry of the night hours
Who always watches and waits
Like a wart on the nose
Even while you snore

O sing
Little Jesus in the wilderness
Carrying the sins of the house
Into every dish, the hated one

O sing
Scupper-tyke, whip-lobber
Smutty-guts, pot-goblin
Garret-whacker, rick-lark
Sump-swab, cupboard-adder

Bobby-robin, knacker-knocker
Sneak-nicker, sprinty-dinty
Pintle-bum

## The Rook

With his clothes-peg beak and his bald face
The Rook tramples all over my place.

He's no beauty. His face is actually
A sort of bleached callus, all scaly

Worn with plunging his beak up to the peepers
Down between earth-clods for crawlers and creepers.

He also pulls up the seed those creatures clutch
Just as it's starting to sprout – and that is such

Vandalism I go with my gun.
Seventy rooks whirl up but down comes one.

So now he'll swing from a stick and with both arms
Signpost his tribe to move on, to different farms.

## Rooks

Rooks love excitement. When I walked in under the
    rookery
A gale churned the silvery, muscular boughs of the beeches,
    and the wet leaves streamed –
It was like a big sea heaving through wreckage –

And the whole crew of rooks lifted off with a shout and
    floated clear.
I could see the oiled lights in their waterproofs
As the blue spilled them this way and that, and their cries
    stormed.

Were they shouting at me? What did they fear?
It sounded

More like a packed football stadium, at the shock of a
   longed-for goal –

A sudden upfling of everything, a surfing cheer.


## The Fox is a Jolly Farmer

The Fox is a jolly farmer and we farm the same land
He's a hardworking farmer, with a farmer's hard hand.

In the corn he farms hares – and what wallopers he rears!
And he plans his poultry system while a-feeling their ears.

In the pond he farms ducks, and a few Christmas geese.
He's an eye for their meat, for their down, for their grease.

In the hayfield it's marvellous the flocks of his voles
And everywhere in the hedges fat rats in their holes.

And everywhere in the hedges, partridges lay clutches
Of eggs for his collection, and some he lets hatch. He's

A hardworking farmer and we farm the same ground.
In our copse he tills rabbits worth many a pound,

And sometimes a cash-crop of squawking young crows.
In the old wood it's beetles he lifts with his nose.

And out on the pasture he borrows my rams,
And my pedigree ewes, for his pedigree lambs.


## The Problem about Lambs

The problem about lambs
Is that each lamb
Is a different jigsaw – and each piece
Is a different problem.

Getting born – one problem
Of many little pieces. The Lamb has to solve it
In the dark, with four fingers.

Once he's born – it's a case
Of which problem comes first. His mother won't have him.
Or he's deficient and won't cooperate.
Or he gets joint-ill
Which sneaks in through the little wick of his umbilical
    cord before it dries up –
Arthritis for infants.

After that comes Orf – known as Lewer.
Ulcers of the nose, of the lips, of the eyes, of the toes,
All at once,
As you read about in the Bible.

Awful things waiting for lambs.

As he grows
Just trotting about gives him footrot. That is, his hooves
    fall apart
Exactly like rotten mussels,
And the cure is to cut them back to the quick and the
    blood
With a knife.

His fleece is for Scab. For Ticks. For Keds. And for Itch-
    mites.
If God gave the sheep her fleece
Why didn't he clean it? Well, I have to clean it
And a right job it is.

Everything makes him cough. Just plain eating
Gives him Fluke. Who invented the Fluke?
It looks like the Fluke of an anchor.
Where was God dozing when he let the Fluke
Anchor in the Lamb?

Then his back end for maggots.
The blowfly is Beelzebub. Maggots are his imps.
God I think forgot sheep altogether.
Sheep is a cruel puzzle of problems.

Brain – what looks just like brainlessness
Is a one-track genius

For roaming, for searching out new pastures,
Always somebody else's,

For unravelling weak places in hedges
And producing a fine clear gap
With a deep trench of tramplings going straight through it.

Sheep is a machine
Of problems
For turning the Shepherd grey as a sheep.


# Sheep (1)

If the world were a Sheep, would the Sheep be its Lamb?
The Sheep is a soft sort of rock
For moonlight and sunlight and rain
Quarried from the world's sheepishness.

The Sheep is a small inland sea,
A wave on four legs,
A living foam, with a heart for a fish
And blood of real sea-water, and half-moon eyes.

The Sheep is a mobile heaven, it nibbles the hill,
A manageable cloud,
A cloud for a lawn, or a field-corner.
A small, patient cloud
In whose shade the Shepherd's dog can rest.
A cloud going nowhere,
Growing on the hillside, fading from it –
A cloud who teaches quiet.

And the Lamb is a flower –
A flower of the snow.
Fearing nothing, like a flake of the snow
That falls on the Iceberg,

And loving the tops of everything, just like the snow,
Dreadful crags and ledges, just like the snow,
Yet loving the sun, too.
A warm flower, an armful of blossom.

And inside the warm lamb-flower
Is a whole constellation
Of stars of water

And the cry of the lamb-flower, such a melting cry,
Is its dark root
In its cloud mother

Who looks like an old ewe.


## Sheep (II)

The Truth about the Sheep alas
Is that it leads a childish life
Head in the fairy-tale of grass
And never thinks about the knife.

They leap when shearers shave them bare.
'Look, we're lambs again,' they bleat.
But their lambs lament and stare
'First you were wool but now you're meat!'

Heavy harvests on the trot
Bags of cash that sit in clover
Where would Sheep be if they were not?
Sheep would long ago be over.


## The Beggarly Bat

The beggarly Bat, a cut-out, scattily
Begs at the lamp's light
A lit moth-mote.

What wraps his shivers?
Scraps of moon cloth
Snatched off cold rivers.

Scissored bits
Of the moon's fashion-crazes
Are his disguises
And wrap up his fits –

For the jittery bat's
Determined to burst
Into day, like the sun

But he never gets past
The dawn's black posts

As long as night lasts
The shuttlecock Bat
Is battered about
By the rackets of ghosts.


## Buzzard

Big hands – broad, workaday hands.
Are they darkened with working the land?
When does he work?
Whoever saw him do anything?

Most of the day he elongates a telephone pole
With his lighthouse look-out and swivel noddle –
He looks more like a moth, crawled up there, owlish,
A furry night-creature of lichen,
Dazed by the sun and wind, clinging and waiting.

Or you see him sitting mid-field
Always doing nothing.
Listening to tangled tales by mole and by bee
And by soft-headed dandelion.

Or he mooches along the old hedgebanks,
Flap-rags, unemployable,
A bit touched in the head. Sometimes
By pure chance he steps on a baby rabbit –
Then he looks like an old Granny
Trying to get her knickers off.
                                        O beggared eagle!

O down-and-out falcon! Up!
Let's see you up there – up! Up!
That's better!

Now let your flags unfurl,
Mew at the sun – give us that eagle feeling!

He floats,
Or he swims – a very slow butterfly-stroke,
Stretching up for the blue. But so lazy!

Finally, he just lets the sky
Bend and hold him aloft by his wing-tips.

There he hangs, dozing off in his hammock.

Mother earth reaches up for him gently.


## A Riddle

Who
Wears the smartest evening dress in England?
Checks his watch by the stars
And hurries, white-scarfed,
To the opera
In the flea-ridden hen-house

Where he will conduct the orchestra?

Who
With a Robin Hood mask over his eyes
Meets King Pheasant the Magnificent
And with silent laughter
Shakes all the gold out of his robes
Then carries him bodily home
Over his shoulder,
A swag-bag?

And who
Flinging back his Dracula cloak
And letting one fang wink in the moonlight
Lifts off his top hat
Shows us the moon through the bottom of it
Then brings out of it, in a flourish of feathers,

The gander we locked up at sunset?

# Pig

The Pig that ploughs the orchard with her nose
Returns
Strutting in her tiny tutu.

The Pig that lies unearthed out there, a giant potato,
Or snores in the straw, an eyeless, legless
Water-bed of wobble and quake,
Can sprint faster than you can.

The sow fallen out there, cratered in mud,
Like the circus fat lady
Fallen off her tightrope, is not happy.
She wants to be a real lady.

The Pig that peers up at you, with blubbery nose
And eyes red from weeping
Wants to be you.

And the lean weaner, with his sawn-off shotgun grin,
Squints his little Judas eye at you.
Oh he's wicked! He burps laughter!
A flea
Earthquakes the world of pig.
And he's splitting at the seams
To keep in the explosion of laughter.
His eyelids screw down tight, keeping it in.
He wants to be a naughty comedian.

The big boar has problems
With the battered swill-buckets of his ears.
He keeps trying to arrange them over his eyes.
Like big poppy petals, but they're too floppy.
I know I'm no beauty, he says. I live for my children.

And the piglets, in elevens and thirteens,
Galloping like apples poured from a barrel,
Flogging themselves with their ears,
Trying to escape from their tails
Cry: Take us with you, take us with you.

All pine for the day they will be people.

# Swallows (I)

Blue splinters of queer metal are swallows,
Magnetized along weird lines of magnetic force –
So they go,
Slide along, hardly a wing-beat, sparkling.

Not mad like swifts. Flight like writing,
Foreign sort of sky-writing – Arabic –
A scrolling, swirling sort of hand –
Everything a signature and a flourish.

There's a heat-wave in swallows –
Dry static of the baked air crackling
Off their wing-tips, and no let-up, round and
Round and round the sun-struck dizzy buildings.

There's thunder too in swallows.
Glitter-dark, flickering over the white hay
Where the flies hide from the lightning
When the air tightens, and the whole sky sags
    low like a big, warm drop.


# Swallows (II)

What is loveliest about swallows
Is the moment they come,
The moment they dip in, and are suddenly there.

For months you just never thought about them
Then suddenly you see one swimming maybe out there
Over our bare tossing orchard, in a slattery April blow,
Probably among big sloppy snowflakes.

And there it is – the first swallow,
Flung and frail – like a midge caught in the waterskin
On the weir's brink – and straightaway you lose it.
You just got a glimpse of whisker and frailty

Then there's nothing but jostled daffodils, like the girls
    running in from a downpour
Shrieking and giggling and shivering,
And the puckered primrose posies, and the wet grit.
It's only a moment, only a flicker, easy to miss –

That first swallow just swinging in your eye-corner
Like a mote in the wind-smart,
A swallow pinned on a roller of air that roars and snatches
    it away
Out of sight, and booms in the bare wood

And you know there'll be colder nights yet
And worse days and you think
'If he's here, there must be flies for him,'
And you think of the flies and their thin limbs in that cold.


## Swallows (III)

I agree
There's nothing verminous, or pestilential, about swallows.
Swallows are the aristocrats
The thoroughbreds of summer.
Still, there is something sinister about them.
I think it's their futuristic design.
The whole evolution of aircraft
Has been to resemble swallows more and more closely.
None of that putt-putting biplane business
Of partridges and pheasants,
Or even the spitfire heroics of hawks.
When I was a boy I remember
Their shapes always alarmed me, slightly,
With the thought of the wars to come,
The speed beyond sound, the molten forms.
You might say
They have a chirruppy chicken-sweet expression,
With goo-goo starlet wide-apart eyes,
And their bills seem tiny, almost retroussé cute –

In fact, the whole face opens
Like a jet engine.

And before that, they solved the problem, did they not,
Of the harpoon?


## Swallows (IV)

I'll say this for swallows, they're marvellous workers.
You think they're sunning by the pond – but no!
They're down there gathering balls of mud – in their
    mouths!
They're building their huts with their beaks!

You see them looping all the directions of the compass
Into a floral bow, and all day
It looks like skater's truant play. It is not.
It's full-tilt, all-out labour, stoking their nestful.

You'd think they'd play a bit, after, with their family –
All figure-flying together. No – they stick at it.
Brood after brood – right up to Michaelmas
The crib's a quiverful of hungry arrows.

They must go round the whole globe twenty times
Just among my buildings. Marvellous!
The truest, keenest, bluest blade-metal,
Whetted on air, every move smoother –

The finest tool on the farm!


## Donkey

My donkey
Is an ancient colour. He's the colour
Of a prehistoric desert
Where great prehistoric suns have sunk and burned out
To a blueish powder.

He stood there through it all, head hanging.

He's the colour
Of a hearth-full of ashes, next morning,
Tinged with rusty pink.

Or the colour of a cast-iron donkey, roasted in a bonfire,
And still standing there after it, cooling,
Pale with ashes and oxides.

He's been through a lot.

But here he is in the nettles, under the chestnut leaves,
With his surprising legs,
Such useful ready legs, so light and active.

And neat round hooves, for putting down just anywhere,
Ready to start out again this minute scrambling all over
    Tibet!

And his quite small body, tough and tight and useful,
Like traveller's luggage,
A thing specially made for hard use, with no trimmings,
Nearly ugly. Made to outlast its owner.

His face is what I like.
And his head, much too big for his body – a toy head,
A great, rabbit-eared, pantomime head,
And his friendly rabbit face,
His big, friendly, humorous eyes – which can turn wicked,
Long and devilish, when he lays his ears back.

But mostly he's comical – and that's what I like.
I like the joke he seems
Always just about to tell me. And the laugh,
The rusty, pump-house engine that cranks up laughter
From some long-ago, far-off, laughterless desert –

The dry, hideous guffaw
That makes his great teeth nearly fall out.

# Pigeons

Pigeons! They're problems. You know why their crop's
   called a crop?
It's where my harvest goes, goes, goes without stop.

Pudgy pests! Prime pods packed with my profit!
They pitch on my farm only for what they pinch off it.

Proper piratical poachers! And what do they pay?
A splintery pigeon pie at the end of the day.


# Bees

At a big wedding
The bees are busy.
Everywhere there are bridesmaids
Almost brides.

And the air
All round the May hive
Twangs
Dangerously. Missiles.

Gingery gleams
Aslant through the ashpoles –
Telegrams
Coming in.

The bees fall
On to their knees, and humbly head-down crawl
Into their crammed church
Where they are fattening

With earth's root-sweetness
A pale idol, many-breasted,
Made of wax. The One
Who'll make their swarm immortal.

The orchard is dizzy with bells.
Everything is tearful. The fumbling, mumbling

Priestly bee, in a shower of petals,
Glues Bride and Groom together with honey.


## Main thing about Badgers

Main thing about badgers is hating daylight.
Funny kind of chap snores all day
In his black hole – sort of root
A ball of roots a potato or a bulb maybe
A whiskery bulb he loves bulbs he'll do a lot to get a good
   bulb
Worms beetles things full of night
Keeping himself filled up with night
A big beetle wobbling along nose down in the mould
Heavy weight of night in him
Heavy pudding of night solid in him and incredibly heavy
Soaking out through his beetle-black legs
Leaving the hair-tips on his bristly back drained empty
And white and his face drained stark white
A ghost mask really a fright mask I know night-shift
   miners
Are very pale but he's whitewashed

Like a sprout's white I suppose underground
He sprouts his nose slowly
Surprising to see it sticking out of the ground
To sniff if the sun's gone – soon he comes rolling out
A fat bulb with a sniffing sprout, a grey mushroom
Just bulging out of the ground and sitting there on top of it
Scratching his fleas sniffing for stars

His sniffing around is a bit like a maggot
Then he's off following his sniff
With his burglar's mask on and his crowbar
Under his moonlight cloak
And all night he's breaking and entering
Dead logs wasps' nests hedgehogs, old wild man of the
   woods in his woad
Crashing about, humming to himself

Amazing physique he has Eskimo wrestler
Really like a Troll bristly gristly
Armpits like an orang-outang when you examine him
And a ridge on his skull like a gorilla
Packed in muscle a crash-helmet of muscle
His head is actually one terrific muscle
With a shocking chomp and sleepy little eyes
To make it seem harmless. But he's harmless enough
Even if he acts guilty. And he makes you smile
When you see his back-end bobbing along in the
    dawn-dew
With the sack of himself bouncing on his gallop
Just like a sack of loot. My Dad said
Kill a badger kill your granny. Kill a badger never see
The moon in your sleep. And so it is.
They disappear under their hill but they work a lot inside
    people.


## The Treecreeper

On a tree-bole, a zigzag upward rivulet
Is a dodgy bird, a midget ace
Busy as a shrew, moth-modest as lichen.

Inchmeal medical examination
Of the tree's skin. Snapshot micro-scanner
And a bill of instant hypodermic.

He's unzipping the tree-bole
For more intimate scrutiny. It sticks. Jerks.
No microbe dare be, nor bubble spider.

All the trees are waiting, pale, undressed,
So he can't dawdle. He jabs, dabs, checks essentials,
Magnet-safe on undersides, then swings

In a blur of tiny machinery
To the next patient's foot, and trickles upwards,
Murmuring 'Good, good!' and 'Good, good!'

Into the huge, satisfying mass of work.

## Weasel (1)

The Weasel whizzes through the woods, he sizzles through
   the brambles.
Compared to him a rabbit hobbles and a whippet ambles.

He's all the heads of here and there, he spins you in a
   dither,
He's peering out of everywhere, his ten tails hither thither.

The Weasel never waits to wonder what it is he's after.
It's butchery he wants, and BLOOD, and merry belly
   laughter.

That's all, that's all, it's no good thinking he's a darling
   creature.
Weight for weight he's twice a tiger, which he'd like to
   teach you.

A lucky thing we're giants! It can't be very nice
Dodging from the Weasel down the mazes of the mice.


## Mouse

The Mouse's round and round and abouts
Bind the whole farm secretly together.
The cat brings in the bitten knots of the string.

The Mouse's sweet look, so intense
Like a young prodigy
Girl violinist, raises the tone of the parlour.

The Mouse in the kitchen, bouncing ping-pong
Among footballing boots, dumb with panic
Lets the silly skirts do the squealing.

While the family sleeps like sacks of turnips
The Mouse, trembling, pop-eyed, solitary,
Braves the ghost.

The Mouse who has watched from his crannies
Everybody's secret and told nobody,
Steals all night with a good conscience.


## Mice are Funny Little Creatures

Mice are funny little creatures
                        you nearly don't see them
Getting out so fast under the sacks more like a bird's
    shadow
Amazing living like that on fearful lightning
Funny too how they smell like lions did you ever smell
    lions in a zoo?

You see one come tottering out
When maybe you're just sitting quiet and he'll come right
    out
With his nose-end wriggling investigating
Every speck of air he seems to be – high on his trembly legs
Very long legs really and his queer little pink hands
Little monkey's hands very human I always think
And his wiry bent tail high up there behind him
Wavering about he looks to be on a tightrope
Then he finds something and starts trembling over it
His nibbling is an all over trembling, his whole body
Trembles as if he were starving and couldn't wait
But it's really listening, he's listening for danger – so
    sensitive
He's trembling it's like a tenderness
So many things can hurt him
And his ears thin as warm wax you've squeezed between
    your finger and thumb
Always remind me of an elephant's ears
A bit shapeless and his long face really like an elephant
If he had a trunk he'd be a tiny elephant exact
At least his face would and his tail being a kind of trunk at
    the wrong end
And his feet being so opposite to great elephant's feet

Help remind you of elephants altogether he really is like an
   elephant
Except his size of course but that reminds you of elephants
   too
Because it's the opposite end of the animals
Like they say extremes meet I can understand
Why mice frighten elephants but they're dear little things
I don't mind what they nibble

## The Fly

The Fly
Is the Sanitary Inspector. He detects every speck
With his Geiger counter.
Detects it, then inspects it
Through his multiple spectacles. You see him everywhere
Bent over his microscope.

He costs nothing, needs no special attention,
Just gets on with the job, totting up the dirt.

All he needs is a lick of sugar
Maybe a dab of meat –
Which is fuel for his apparatus.
We never miss what he asks for. He can manage
With so little you can't even tell
Whether he's taken it.

In his black boiler suit, with his gas-mask,
His oxygen pack,
His crampons,
He can get anywhere, explore any wreckage,
Find the lost –

Whatever dies – just leave it to him.
He'll move in
With his team of gentle undertakers,
In their pneumatic protective clothing, afraid of nothing,
Little white Michelin men,
They hoover up the rot, the stink, and the goo.

He'll leave you the bones and the feathers – souvenirs
Dry-clean as dead sticks in the summer dust.

Panicky people misunderstand him –
Blitz at him with nerve-gas puff-guns,
Blot him up with swatters.

He knows he gets filthy.
He knows his job is dangerous, wading in the drains
Under cows' tails, in pigs' eye-corners
And between the leaky broken toes
Of the farm buildings –
He too has to cope with the microbes.
He too wishes he had some other job.
But this is his duty
Just let him be. Let him rest on the wall there,
Scrubbing the back of his neck. This is his rest-minute.

Once he's clean, he's a gem.

A freshly barbered sultan, royally armoured
In dusky rainbow metals.

A knight on a dark horse.

Flies

I don't know about flies.

I don't like to see a fly
Wandering about in the air
Outside a rabbit-hole, then going in.
Somebody's died down there.

I don't like to see a fly
Tapping the eye ball
And peering into the eye
Of a cow stretched out in her stall.

And I hate to feel a fly
When I'm taking a snooze after lunch
Walk to my mouth-corner –
As if just checking a hunch.

## Weasel (II)

Every creature in its own way
Mistakes the Weasel
For somebody else – too late.

The Weasel's white chest
Is the pretty pinafore of the waitress
Who brings the field-vole knife and fork.

The Weasel's black ripe eyes
Brim with a heady elderberry wine
That makes the Rat drunk.

The Weasel's fully-fashioned coat,
Lion-colour, wins her admittance
To the club of snobby goslings.

When the Weasel dances her belly dance
Brainless young buck rabbits
Simpering, go weak at the knees.

When the Weasel laughs
Even the Mole sees the joke
And rolls in the aisles, helpless.


## The White-Collared Dove

O the White-Collared Dove has a swollen nose!
His head is nipped thin for his eyes are too close.
And the blood in his eye is as pink as his toes!

He has an acrobatic stunt – in April
He bounces up an invisible rigging in the air
And with a toppling clap of his wings
Launches off at the top, like a wide-armed free-fall diver.

Sometimes he goes up so steep and crazy
Clapping his wings at the height he almost
Comes over backwards.

That  makes his betrothed go hot and cold.

She's watching from the ash. He corkscrews down
To breathe in her ear –
His throat is plummy,
Some peacock on his nape,
A ruffle of silks – a rippling

It's the flame inside there, playing on the metals,
The voice in there, the muffled bellows
That swells the oaks, that splits the chestnut's wrappers –

There are bells in the blue haze and soft brass bands
At a Sunday distance, but only wood pigeons
Breathe on the embers that make summer simmer –

'Who woos? Both of us,'
Or 'Who woos? You do,'
Or just 'Who woos – me –'

The weathercock melts.


## The Roustabout Rooster

Why is it
The roustabout Rooster, raging at the dawn
Wakes us so early?

A warrior-king is on fire!
His armour is all crooked daggers and scimitars
And it's shivering red-hot – with rage!

And he screams out through his megaphone:
'Give me back my Queens!'

What's happened?

He fell asleep, a King of Tropic India
With ten thousand concubines, each one
Gorgeous as a volcanic sunset –

But now he wakes, turned inside out – a rooster!
With eleven flea-bitten hens!

And he remembers it all. No wonder he screeches:
'Give me back my Queens!'

No wonder his scarlet cheeks vibrate like a trumpet!

But it's no use. He seems to droop.
It's simply no use.
All that majestic armour is just feathers.

But now it comes over him again!
Again he goes all stiff – and quivering!
He aims himself at the sun.
He looks like a flame-thrower,
And with one blast, as if it were his last,
Tries to turn himself back outside in
With: 'Give me back my Queens!'

The sun yawns and saunters away among some clouds.
The empty-headed hens
Are happy unriddling the cinders.
Only the cockerel dreams and trembles and flames.


Hen


The Hen
Worships the dust. She finds God everywhere.
Everywhere she finds his jewels.
And she does not care
What the cabbage thinks.

She has forgotten flight
Because she has interpreted happily
Her recurrent dream
Of clashing cleavers, of hot ovens,
And of the little pen-knife blade
Splitting her palate.
She flaps her wings, like shallow egg-baskets,
To show her contempt
For those who live on escape
And a future of empty sky.

She rakes, with noble, tireless foot,
The treasury of the dirt,
And clucks with the mechanical alarm clock
She chose instead of song
When the Creator
Separated the Workers and the Singers.

With her eye on reward
She tilts her head religiously
At the most practical angle
Which reveals to her
That the fox is a country superstition,
That her eggs have made man her slave
And that the heavens, for all their threatening,
Have not yet fallen.

And she is stern. Her eye is fierce – blood
(That weakness) is punished instantly.
She is a hard bronze of uprightness.
And indulges herself in nothing
Except to swoon a little, a delicious slight swoon,
One eye closed, just before sleep,
Conjuring the odour of tarragon.

## Goat

A few quick flirts of their shameless tails –
Each tail looks like a whiskery woodlouse
Jerking to attention – and every rose fails.

And their triangular, axe-shaped, munching heads
Seem to say – looking at me cock-eyed –
Funny, your young apple trees have all just died.

A plague out of the Old Testament are goats!
Satan, sitting in their throats,
Looks at me through their evil eyes and gloats.

When a goat pulls at your coat, it's a sampling bite.
There it stands, chewing its marble, thinking:
I'll gnaw this whole globe down to a meteorite!

## Billy Goat

With a watery trickle of hooves, a tender bleating,
Nose to the grindstone, working at eating,
Round the Mediterranean Sea
With all his family
The Billy Goat passed
Like a nuclear blast.

Out of the dusty fall of Babylon the Great
Walked the Goat, still searching for something to eat.

Out of the tombs of Egypt stepped forth
The Goat, chewing a scrap of mummy cloth.

Into the cave, from which Christ's body had flown,
The Goat peered, evil-eyed, with his horns on.

Whenever a goat stops eating
And aims at you with his nose
Remember the deserts waiting
Between his dirty toes.

## Nanny Goat

If the Goat's eye really were a globe
    all of pale, iceberg-haunted sea,
If the Goat's eye really were the tip of an icicle
    forming in a cold rusty furnace,
If the Goat's eye really had moved, suddenly,
    in the face of the statue of a stone god
    dug up in a desert

Though the Goat's dainty lips
    are a kind of dryish sea-anemone
Though the Goat's mean lips
    are the leaves of a thorn on a blustery
      headland
And though the Goat's front legs

are the ballet of spray flung higher up the
            cliff
        seeming to cling there
        while it nibbles the buds
And though the Goat's hooves are
        the first rattle of the stones on your coffin
And though the Goat's hairs truly are
        fallen from a constellation
        a stray greasy starlight, radioactive with chaos
Into the milking bowl

The Nanny Goat's milk is still the sweetest of milks

And her cheese of cheeses


## Geese

Geese are godly creatures, not just for Christmas show.
At my first note on their bucket, though it's ten degrees
    below,
Their choir stands in a ring and they lift their throats of
    snow.

And they carol out their discords, till their tall necks fence
    me in
With a rusty-shipyard bonging echoing hollow din.
Noël, Noël, they clang to God, which can't be called a sin.

Devil's feet of lizard leather! Wrangling, squirmy necks!
Hissing cauldrons! Haggish witches gabbling out a hex!
It's only the gander warning you from his wives with a
    threat of pecks –

The ladies laugh their loony laughter, gossiping together,
Or arguing about a puddle, or a duck's feather.
Or they remember the white seas and the snows of polar
    weather

And all begin to sing, and stretch up as if to fly
At a sudden vision of icebergs, and they yodel out a cry
That cannons between iron mountains and an iron sky –

But all fall like snow. It is sad, but it must be.
I sit and bare the breast of down, the weight across my
    knee,
And I'm ankle-deep in the whiteness, and the fluff goes
    floating free,

Till the poor body's nude as a babe, except for the neck
    and head,
The neck in its muff, its ruff of plumes, pretending to be
    dead,
But the bright eye still open hearing every word that's said,

And the beak that worked so hard at the world, and sang
    to me so strong,
Holding carefully silent the plump tip of its tongue
Lest it spoil our Christmas Feast with any whisper of
    wrong.


## Two Geese

I remember two geese – mainly remember
The muck they waddled in – you wouldn't dare
Tread there, under sad apple trees.
Two dirty queens, hating each other.

They couldn't fly to the ice-floes. Did they ever see snow
    fuming
Off sun-dazzle peaks? Their necks had long lost
The poured cream of a goose's plump neck softness.
Instead, clutching their draggly bunched-up skirts,

Lifting out of mud bare feet that were
More like rubber frogfeet, these two queens
Held their noses high – blue eyes always
Peering over something – or bowed, studying

Mud for another egg. Bub, bub, bub!
Nowhere to put their load of dirty laundry,
Each foot going down like a paint-brush – sploodge!
Sploodge! Sploodge! – wobble weighty,

Not quite tripping up at each step,
Sagging their keels. A toppling pyramid
Of sixty or more
Mudded, rain-cold, probably rotten eggs,

Under the wall, was the addled castle
Each of them seemed to be trying to own.
Odd eggs lay everywhere – cannonballs
Of their miserable battle – abandoned

Where they'd rolled. Though these geese were queens,
That was a prison yard, and they were convicts,
And their punishment was to go on laying eggs
And to go on stealing each other's eggs

And never know they were spellbound. It was April.
Sunlight peered through the wall.
One jabbed at a muddy stub-end of cabbage.
One sat back in the armchair of herself,

A little smoke of down stirred in her nostril.


## The Vixen

An October robin kept
Stringing its song
On gossamer that snapped.
The weir-pool hung
Lit with honey leaves.
Ploughed hills crisp as loaves

In the high morning.
I waded the river's way
Body and ear leaning
For whatever the world might say
Of the word in her womb
Curled unborn and dumb.

Still as the heron
I let the world grow near
With a ghostly salmon

Hanging in thin air
So real it was holy
And watching seemed to kneel.

And there I saw the vixen
Coiled on her bank porch.
Her paws were bloody sticks.
Ears on guard for her searchers
She had risked a sleep
And misjudged how deep.


## Hunting Song

O he steals our crooked speeches, says the Hunting Horn,
    Steals our slanders and our lies
    Which are demons in disguise,
And he nails them to his tongue, so it hangs out pink and
  long,
And he flees us like a robber, says the Hunting Horn.

And he steals out of our souls all the popping fiery coals
    Our malice and suspicion
    Which are devils in perdition,
And he nails them to his ears, where they can't be
  quenched by tears,
And he flees us like a robber, says the Hunting Horn.

And he steals out of our throats the greediness that gloats
    On the muttons, beefs and porks
    That weep upon our forks,
And he nails it in his grin, where the wind blows out and in,
And he flees us like a robber, says the Hunting Horn.

And he steals our wicked blood and he rides it through the
  mud,
    The mare of blood that bears us,
    The red hunter that wears us,
And it's like a witch's stick that he rides through thin and
  thick
As he flees us like a robber, says the Hunting Horn.

And he's nailed our fear of darkness to his four paws
	dipped in quickness,
		Our cowardice a nail
		In the white tip of his tail,
With the limestone from our hearts, he's whitewashed his
	underparts,
And he flees us like a robber, says the Hunting Horn.

Then in a belling applause of hounds, he bounds off the
	earth and leaves no traces –
Just as if we'd washed our hands and faces.


## Worms

I hear for every acre there's a ton of worms beneath.
I hear that worm-meat's better meat than fatted barley
	beef.
We're farming only half our farms, and that's the new
	belief.

I think I'm growing barley, bullocks, pigs and lambs
	galore.
From six a.m. till nine at night I toil my body sore.
But I'm only feeding the roots of the worms, it's worms I'm
	working for.

Below my clover meadows worms are bellowing in the
	dark.
They're bound for nobody's oven, one or two might go to
	the lark.
They gobble their way through the earth's black pudding
	safe as they were in the ark.

Worms riot and revel in their rude and naked hordes.
And most of what I fatten, far, far more than my farm
	affords
Falls into their idle mouths, and the whole lot live like
	lords.

## Weasel (III)

Its face is a furry lizard's face, but prettier.

Only the Weasel
Is wick as a weasel.
Whipping whisk

Of a grim cook. And a lit trail
Of gunpowder, he fizzes
Toward a shocking stop.

His tail jaunts along for the laughs.

His grandfather, to keep him active,
Buried the family jewels
Under some rabbit's ear.

Tyrannosaur – miniaturized
To slip through every loop-hole
In the laws of rats and mice.

Terrorist
Of the eggs –

Over the rim of the thrush's nest
The Weasel's face, bright as the Evening Star,
Brings night.

# Catching Carp

When the heat-wave world of midsummer
Is set out to cool, in the oven mouth,
After sundown,

The pond
Wobbles, as if the bed of it, at one corner
Were still on a red ring.

Bats shiver. The western sky
Cools its powdery crucible colours.
It's a midsummer madness. Crouching

To catch a great carp is how I imagine
Gold-fever. And right at your feet, maybe,
Earth will suddenly open –

A bullion chest will heave up
Streaming with lilies, and roll over
And you'll grab at it –
Maybe you'll glimpse a spill of doubloons
As it slides under again, too heavy.

Then the pond weltering. The first star
Molten and writhing.
     And you're left

Silver-plated

A glistening piece of the treasure

As the moon climbs up your back.

# The Twilight White Owl

To see the twilight white Owl wavering over the dew-mist
Startles my heart, a mouse in its house,
   remembering a dim past

When we were only the weight of shrews, maybe, and
   everything ate us
In a steaming, echoing jungle of night-flying alligators,

And the dawn-chorus shook the swamps, a booming
   orchestra
Where Brontosaurs were merely the flutes, and land-whales
   beat on the drum of the ear –

It has all sunk into the fern-fringed forest pool of the Owl's
   eye,
But it reaches over the farm like a claw in the Owl's
   catspaw cry.

The Owl sways, weighing the hushed world, his huge gaze
   dry and light
As a blown dandelion clock, or the moon-husk of the
   oldest night.


# The Hare (1)

That Elf
Riding his awkward pair of haunchy legs

That weird long-eared Elf
Wobbling down the highway

Don't overtake him, don't try to drive past him,
He's scatty, he's all over the road,
He can't keep his steering, in his ramshackle go-cart,
His big loose wheels, buckled and rusty,
Nearly wobbling off

And all the screws in his head wobbling and loose
And his eyes wobbling

# The Hare (II)

The Hare is a very fragile thing.
The life in the hare is a glassy goblet, and her yellow-
   fringed frost-flake belly says: Fragile.
The hare's bones are light glass. And the hare's face –

Who lifted her face to the Lord?
Her new-budded nostrils and lips,
For the daintiest pencillings, the last eyelash touches
Delicate as the down of a moth,
And the breath of awe
Which fixed the mad beauty-light
In her look
As if her retina
Were a moon perpetually at full.

Who is it, at midnight on the A30,
The Druid soul,
The night-streaker, the sudden lumpy goblin
That thumps the car under the belly
Then cries with human pain
And becomes a human baby on the road
That you dare hardly pick up?

Or leaps, like a long bat with little headlights,
Straight out of darkness
Into the driver's nerves
With a jangle of cries
As if the car had crashed into a flying harp

So that the driver's nerves flail and cry
Like a burst harp.

# The Hare (III)

Uneasy she nears
As if she were being lured, but fearful,

Nearer.
Like a large egg toppling itself – mysterious!

Then she'll stretch, tall, on her hind feet,
And lean on the air,
Taut – like a stilled yacht waiting on the air –

And what does the hunter see? A fairy woman?
A dream beast?
A kangaroo of the March corn?

The loveliest face listening,
Her black-tipped ears hearing the bud of the blackthorn
Opening its lips,
Her black-tipped hairs hearing tomorrow's weather
Combing the mare's tails,
Her snow-fluff belly feeling for the first breath,
Her orange nape, foxy with its dreams of the fox –

Witch-maiden
Heavy with trembling blood – astounding
How much blood there is in her body!
She is a moony pond of quaking blood

Twitched with spells, her gold-ringed eye spellbound –

Carrying herself so gently, balancing
Herself with the gentlest touches
As if her eyes brimmed –


## The Hare (IV)

I've seen her,
A lank, lean hare, with her long thin feet
And her long, hollow thighs,
And her ears like ribbons
Careering by moonlight
In her Flamenco, her heels flinging the dust
On the drum of the hill.

And I've seen him, hobbling stiffly
God of Leapers

Surprised by dawn, earth-bound, and stained
With drying mud,
Painfully rocking over the furrows
With his Leaping-Legs, his Power-Thighs
Much too powerful for ordinary walking,
So powerful
They seem almost a burden, almost a problem,
Nearly an aching difficulty for him
When he tries to loiter or pause,
Nearly a heaving pain to lift and move
Like turning a cold car-engine with a bent crank handle –

Till a shock, a terror, with a bang
Grabs at her ears. An oven door
Bangs open, both barrels, and a barking
Bursts out of onions –
                          and she leaps
And her heels
Hard as angle-iron kick salt and pepper
Into the lurcher's gullet –
                          and kick and kick
The spinning, turnip world
Into the lurcher's gullet –
                          as she slips
Between thin hawthorn and thinner bramble
Into tomorrow.

## The Hare (v)

There's something eerie about a hare, no matter how
    stringy and old.
I heard of a hare caught in a snowdrift, brought in under a
    coat from the cold.
Turned by firelight into a tall fine woman who many a
    strange tale told.

The hare has a powerful whiff with her, even when she's a
    pet.

Her back as broad and strong as a dog, and her kick like a
     bull-calf, yet
Into your dreams she waltzes strung with starlight and
     music, a marionette.

They say it's a nude witch dancing her rings though it
     looks like a lolloping hare
Circling the farm, like a full moon circling the globe, and
     leaning to stare
Huge-eyed in at the midnight window down at the sleeping
     children there.

Something scares me about a hare, like seeing an escapee
From a looney-bin, lurching and loping along in his
     flapping pyjamas, free –
Or meeting a woman mad with religion who has fastened
     her eyes on me.

You'll never hurt a hare after you've heard her cry in pain.
A mother's scream, a baby's scream, and a needle slips in
     through your ear and brain
To prick and prick your heart when you even hear of the
     hurt of a hare again.


## Bullfinch

A mournful note, a crying note
A single tin-whistle half-note, insistent
Echoed by another
Slightly bluer with a brief distance
In March, in the draughty, dripping orchard.

And again and again – and the echo prompt.
Bullfinch is melancholy.

Bullfinch wants us to feel a cold air, a shivery sadness
And to pity him in his need,
In the poverty start of the year, the hungry end,

Too early
In his Persian plum-plush wedding regalia
Above bleak, virginal daffodils.

He wants us to feel protective
At least for as long as it takes him
To strip every tree of its bud-blossom –

To pack a summerful of apple-power
Under his flaming shirt.


## Pheasant

I was carrying our cat
Across a ploughed field. Above us, a blue-black piled-up
   sky
Boiled bulgy clouds.
I thought: it's like giant blackberries. And I thought:
If it rains, I'll be a queer colour.

There came a crack of lightning.
It was like being cracked over the skull with a splintering
   bamboo.
The lid flew off everything. I saw the blue-hot centre.
I thought: This is it, a planet's crashed into us.
And our cat was so scared, it peed all warm down my
   shirt.

Then everything was alright again.
Except our cat had turned into some kind of bird
That started struggling to fly. I had to hold it hard.
The thing about this bird
Was it was made of gold.

All soft warm scale-armour, its feathers were scales
And every scale was the flame of a candle
Hammered out flat – part solid, but the gold fringe still
   soft flame,
And I knew these flames were off candles
That angels had held. Suddenly this bird

Burst free and bounced on to the tilth in front of me
And stood there, dishevelled.
Then it shook its flames into shape, it whirled itself

Like a bottleful of bright coins, and stood brighter.
It had horns on its head. And I saw its head

Was a word in Chinese.
I stared into its flame, I couldn't stare into it hard enough.
And I stared at its head –
I knew that word had a meaning
But the meaning was too big, I had to hold my head in

Because I could feel it trying to split.
It was a funny dream all right.
Then my head actually split – the two halves came right
    apart
And the bird was looking at me, I saw its barbed tongue
And it let out a yell, and I woke up –

What I'd heard was a pheasant.


## Dog

I dreamed I woke and was a bark
Working at the postman and the boy
With the newspaper. I watched hard
My master's breakfast mouth,
Sitting with all my might.
With all my skill I caught
The bacon-rind and did for it –
Clapping my chops to make a neat job.
When he stood I was so quick
Already standing, and my tail turning over
Without a problem. On the way
I checked every sniff – Good morning! Good morning!
I even managed a handy bark
At the dog on the next farm, over four fields
And got a good boy for it.
Cows' heels were just starters warming me up –
I could do it with my tongue idling.
Serious at sheep was how I earned my keep
Working my master's face

Through all its shapes, without a mistake,
Getting his arms right each time
And making his whistle easy.
My ears fairly ached
At stopping and starting.
I had every single mutton helpless
Under my ideas.
I threw in a few dodges –
Spinning them on one hoof,
Rolling the flock up on three sides at once
Like a pasty,
Pouring them through a nozzle.
I made a point
Of snatching a good boy
From under the tail of each one.
My panting
Finally used all the work up,
And daylight had to go.
I ate a bowl of good boy
Still keeping my master's eyes safe,
And resting his footsteps in my right ear
Till I slept.
Believe me, I slept without a pause
Even when the sleep-wolf
Jeering at me, dashed through my skin
Like a clock-alarm.


## Somebody

Drip-tree stillness. And a spring-feeling elation
Of mid-morning oxygen. There was a yeasty simmering
Over the land – all compass points were trembling
Bristling with starlings, hordes out of the North,
Bubbly and hopeful.

We stood in the mist-rawness
Of the sodden earth. The Day Before Christmas.
We could hear the grass seeping.

Then a wraith-smoke
Writhed up from a far field and condensed
On a frieze of dwarfish hedge-oaks – sizzling
Like power-pylons in mist.
We eased our way into the landscape.
Casual midnightish draughts, in the soaking stillness.
Itch of starlings was everywhere.
                              Our gun
Was old, rust-ugly, single-barrelled, borrowed
For a taste of English sport. My friend had come
From eighteen years' Australian estrangement
Twelve thousand miles through thin air
To walk again on the tight hills of the West,
In the ruby and emerald glow, the leaf-wet oils
Of his memory's masterpiece.
                              Hedge-sparrows
Needled the bramble-mass undergrowth
With their weepy warnings.
                              He had the gun.
We hardened our eyes. A patrol.
The gun-muzzle was sniffing. And the broad land
Tautened into wider, nervier contrasts
Of living and unliving. Our eyes feathered over it –
It was a touchy detonator. Slow,

Bootprints between the ranks of baby barley
Heel and toe we trod
Narrowed behind the broad gaze of the gun
Down the long woodside. I was the dog.

Now I got into the wood. I pushed parallel
And slightly ahead – the idea
Was to flush something for the gun's amusement.

I go delicate. I don't want to panic
My listeners into a crouch-freeze.
I want them to keep their initiative
And slip away, confident, still careless,
Out across the gun.
                    Pigeons, too far,

Burst up from under the touch
Of our furthest listenings. A bramble
Claws across my knee, and a blackbird
Five yards off explodes its booby-trap
Shattering wetly
Black and yellow alarm-dazzlings, and a long string
Of fireworks down the wood. It settles
To a hacking chatter and that blade-ringing
Like a flint on an axe-head.

                               I wait.

That startled me too.
I know I am a Gulliver now
Tied by my every slightest move
To a thousand fears. But I move –
And a jay, invisibly somewhere safe
Starts pretending to tear itself in half
From the mouth backwards. With three screams
It scares itself to silence.
                         The whole wood
Has hidden in the wood. Its mossy tunnels
Seem to age as I listen. A raven
Dabs a single charcoal toad-croak
Into the finished picture.
                           I come out
To join my friend in the field. We need a new plan
To surprise something.
                      But as I come over the wire
He is pointing, silent.
I look. One hundred yards
Down the woodside, somebody
Is watching us.

A strangely dark fox
Motionless in his robe of office
Is watching us. It is a shock.

Too deep in the magic wood, suddenly
We have met the magician.
                    Then he's away –

A slender figurine, dark and witchy,
A rocking nose-down lollop, and the load of tail
Floating behind him, over the swell of faint corn
Into the long arm of woodland opposite.

The gun does nothing. But we gaze after
Like men who have been given a secret sign.
We are studying the changed expression
Of that straggle of scrub and poor trees
Which is now the disguise of a fox.

And the gun is thinking. The gun
Is working its hunter's magic.
It is transforming us, there in the dull mist,
To two suits of cold armour –
Empty of all but a strange new humming,
A mosquito of primeval excitements.
And as we start to walk out over the field
The gun smiles.

The fox will be under brambles.
He has set up his antennae,
His dials are glowing and quivering,
Every hair adjusts itself
To our coming.
                        Will he wait in the copse
Till we've made our move, as if this were a game
He is interested to play?
Or has he gone through and away over further fields?
Or down and into the blueish mass and secrecy
Of the main wood?

Under a fat oak, where the sparse copse
Joins the main wood, my friend leans in ambush.
Well out in the corn, talking to air
Like quiet cogs, I stroll to the top of the strip –
Pretending to be both of us –
Then pierce the brush, clumsy as a bullock, a trampling
Like purposeless machinery, towards my friend,
Noisy enough for him to know
Where not to point his blind gun.

186  *from* WHAT IS THE TRUTH?

Somewhere between us
The fox is inspecting me, magnified.
And now I tangle all his fears with a silence,
Then a sudden abrupt advance, then again silence,
Then a random change of direction –

And almost immediately,
Almost before I've decided we are serious –
The blast wall hits me, the gun bang bursts
Like a paper bag in my face,
The whole day bursts like a paper bag –
But a new world is created instantly
With no visible change.

I pause. I call. My friend does not answer.
Everything is just as it had been.
The corroded blackberry leaves,
The crooked naked trees, fingering sky
Are all the usual, careful shapes
Of the usual silence.

I go forward. And now I see my friend
As if he had missed,
Leaning against his tree, casual.
But between us, on the tussocky ground,
Somebody is struggling with something.
An elegant gentleman, beautifully dressed,
Is struggling there, tangled with something,
And biting at something
With his flashing mouth. It is himself
He is tangled with. I come close
As if I might be of help.
But there is no way out.
It is himself he is biting,
Bending his head far back, and trying
To bite his shoulder. He has no time for me.
Blood beneath him is spoiling
The magnificent sooted russet
Of his overcoat, and the flawless laundering
Of his shirt. He is desperate
To get himself up on his feet,

And if he could catch the broken pain
In his teeth, and pull it out of his shoulder,
He still has some hope, because
The long brown grass is the same
As it was before, and the trees
Have not changed in any way,
And the sky continues the same –

It is doing the impossible deliberately
To set the gun-muzzle at his chest
And funnel that sky-bursting bang
Down through a sudden blue-pit in his fur
Into the earth beneath him.

He cannot believe it has happened.

His chin sinks forward, and he half-closes his mouth
In a smile
Of incredulous bitterness,
And half-closes his eyes
Into a fineness beyond pain –

And it is a dead fox in the dank woodland.

And I stand awake – as one wakes
From what feels like a cracking blow on the head.
That second shot has ruined his skin.
We chop his tail off
Thick and long as a forearm, and black.
Then bundle him and his velvet legs
His bag of useless jewels,
The phenomenal technology inside his head,
Into a hole, under a bulldozed stump,
Like picnic rubbish. There the memory ends.

We must have walked away.


## Lobworms

O early one dawn I walked over the dew
And I saw a strange thing I will now tell to you.

Where mud had been trampled at a trough by the cattle
Till it looked like the field of the famous Somme battle

I saw two bare creatures, stark naked were they
Full length in the mud, at the dawn of the day.

They were big blue-nosed lobworms who stretched to
    embrace
From their separate dug-outs, in that dreadful place.

O they twisted together like two loving tongues
And they had not a care for the world and its wrongs.

O they clung in a spittle, like passionate lips
From their separate holes, as from separate ships.

And that was a wonder to watch in the dawn
In the world wet with dew, like a garden new-born.

It was Adam and Eve in the earliest light –
And I was like Satan, for they suddenly took fright.

Their loving was chilled at the touch of my stare –
O I almost could hear it, their cry of despair

As like snapping elastic, they whipped back apart
And I can still feel it, the shock and the smart

As they vanished in earth, each alone to its den.
And I've never seen such a marvel again.

## Ants

Can an Ant love an Ant?
Can a scissor-face
Kiss a scissor-face?
Can an Ant smile? It can't.

Why all that coming and going?
They run, they wave their arms, they cry –
The Ants' nest is a nunnery
Of holy madwomen.

They race out, searching for God.
They race home: 'He's not there!'
And their mad heads nod, nod, nod,
And they stagger in despair.

Bicycling, weeping, trembling (once
To have lost your last hope yet to
Still have just a chance
Is enough to know what they go through)

And carrying such a sob
Inside a body that's
Part hard little knots
And part a scalding blob

Of molten copper trickling
Through a burning house.
Love of God is fierce!

But the Sun's great yokel, Earth, only yawns and scratches
   the tickling.


## Spider

On the whole, people dislike spiders.
Where is my book of spiders? A book of devotions
Penned by a passionate heart,
By a dedicated priest of the spider.

The anatomy – so prodigal in wonders!
And the strategies for reproduction,
For gratifying the hungers, beggar belief.
Web-weaving
Is the slightest of the spider's talents
Compared to the feats of prestidigitation
That usher his offspring to their independence.
The web is part acronym, part phone,
Part boutique front for the real business –
A sparkle of his virtuoso wit
Cast over trifles, to beguile fools.

Even so, he's ignorant of his best art,
Which is to dangle, on his invisible harness,
On to my page, from my hair.
Then the thought 'Thank God – I'm in for some luck!'
Really startles me.
And for a whole hour after, I feel much better
And, though he doesn't feel it, I love him.

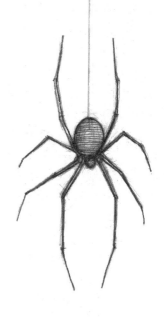

# SEASON SONGS

## A March Calf

Right from the start he is dressed in his best – his blacks
   and his whites.
Little Fauntleroy – quiffed and glossy,
A Sunday suit, a wedding natty get-up,
Standing in dunged straw

Under cobwebby beams, near the mud wall,
Half of him legs,
Shining-eyed, requiring nothing more
But that mother's milk come back often.

Everything else is in order, just as it is.
Let the summer skies hold off, for the moment.
This is just as he wants it.
A little at a time, of each new thing, is best.

Too much and too sudden is too frightening –
When I block the light, a bulk from space,
To let him in to his mother for a suck,
He bolts a yard or two, then freezes,

Staring from every hair in all directions,
Ready for the worst, shut up in his hopeful religion,
A little syllogism
With a wet blue-reddish muzzle, for God's thumb.

You see all his hopes bustling
As he reaches between the worn rails towards
The topheavy oven of his mother.
He trembles to grow, stretching his curl-tip tongue –

What did cattle ever find here
To make this dear little fellow
So eager to prepare himself?
He is already in the race, and quivering to win –

His new purpled eyeball swivel-jerks
In the elbowing push of his plans.
Hungry people are getting hungrier,
Butchers developing expertise and markets,

But he just wobbles his tail – and glistens
Within his dapper profile
Unaware of how his whole lineage
Has been tied up.

He shivers for feel of the world licking his side.
He is like an ember – one glow
Of lighting himself up
With the fuel of himself, breathing and brightening.

Soon he'll plunge out, to scatter his seething joy,
To be present at the grass,
To be free on the surface of such a wideness,
To find himself himself. To stand. To moo.


## The River in March

Now the river is rich, but her voice is low.
It is her Mighty Majesty the sea
Travelling among the villages incognito.

Now the river is poor. No song, just a thin mad whisper.
The winter floods have ruined her.
She squats between draggled banks, fingering her rags and
   rubbish.

And now the river is rich. A deep choir.
It is the lofty clouds, that work in heaven,
Going on their holiday to the sea.

The river is poor again. All her bones are showing.
Through a dry wig of bleached flotsam she peers up
   ashamed
From her slum of sticks.

Now the river is rich, collecting shawls and minerals.
Rain brought fatness, but she takes ninety-nine percent
Leaving the fields just one percent to survive on.

And now she is poor. Now she is East wind sick.
She huddles in holes and corners. The brassy sun gives her
   a headache.
She has lost all her fish. And she shivers.

But now once more she is rich. She is viewing her lands.
A hoard of king-cups spills from her folds, it blazes, it
   cannot be hidden.
A salmon, a sow of solid silver,

Bulges to glimpse it.


## March Morning Unlike Others

Blue haze. Bees hanging in air at the hive-mouth.
Crawling in prone stupor of sun
On the hive-lip. Snowdrops. Two buzzards,
Still-wings, each
Magnetised to the other,
Float orbits.
Cattle standing warm. Lit, happy stillness.
A raven, under the hill,
Coughing among bare oaks.
Aircraft, elated, splitting blue.
Leisure to stand. The knee-deep mud at the trough
Stiffening. Lambs freed to be foolish.

The earth invalid, dropsied, bruised, wheeled
Out into the sun,
After the frightful operation.
She lies back, wounds undressed to the sun,
To be healed,
Sheltered from the sneapy chill creeping North wind,
Leans back, eyes closed, exhausted, smiling
Into the sun. Perhaps dozing a little.
While we sit, and smile, and wait, and know
She is not going to die.

## He Gets Up in Dark Dawn

To misted stillness.
First thrush splutters and chips at the thick light.
Suddenly the room leaps, blue-lit. Was it lightning?
Then the crumplings and the bamboo splittings
In echoey heaven-corridors, of close thunder.

He listens for the rain and it starts.
Taptap on the roof. The birds too,
Gurgling and exercising their highest and their lowest
And all the twisting stairs from one to the other,
Singing in dark holds of young leaves and unopened
   blossoms,
Not knowing who lives in the house, or who has lived,
Or what year this is, or what century this is.

Through thick vapour swaddle
Violet lightning shakes its shutters
And thunder trundles its drums from the highest attic
Of heaven to the lowest, furthest basement.
He stands in the open door and cannot go fishing.

He sits hearing his kettle. Lightning again
Tosses the kitchen, the birds bustle their voices
Squibby-damp, echoless, but not daunted
Out in the nodding, dripping, flickering, blue garden.
The thunder splits and lets its domes collapse.
Ginger, his cat, tenses and rises listening
To the step by step approach of the thunder

As if ghosts were creaking all over the house.
His head sleeks very slender, with ears
That want both to prick listening and to flatten.
Thunder unloads its last stamping arrival
As the lights jump in and out – the sky is falling –
He flattens –

His master explains with quiet, meaningless words.

# Spring Nature Notes

### I

The sun lies mild and still on the yard stones.

The clue is a solitary daffodil – the first.

And the whole air struggling in soft excitements
Like a woman hurrying into her silks.
Birds everywhere zipping and unzipping
Changing their minds, in soft excitements,
Warming their wings and trying their voices.

The trees still spindle bare.

Beyond them, from the warmed blue hills
An exhilaration swirls upward, like a huge fish.

As under a waterfall, in the bustling pool.

Over the whole land
Spring thunders down in brilliant silence.

### II

An oak tree on the first day of April
Is as bare as the same oak in December
But it looks completely different.

Now it bristles, it is a giant brazier
Of invisible glare, an invisible sun.
The oak tree's soul has returned and flames its strength.
You feel those rays – even though you can't see them
They touch you.

(Just as you feel touched, and turn round
To meet eyes staring straight at the back of your head.)

### III

A spurt of daffodils, stiff, quivering –
Plumes, blades, creases, Guardsmen
At attention

Like sentinels at the tomb of a great queen.
(Not like what they are – the advance guard
Of a drunken slovenly army

Which will leave this whole place wrecked.)

### IV

The crocuses are too naked. Space shakes them.
They remind you the North Sky is one vast hole
With black space blowing out of it
And that you too are being worn thin
By the blowing atoms of decomposed stars.

Down the moonbeams come hares
Hobbling on their square wheels.
What space has left, the hares eat.

What the hares do not want
Looks next morning like the leavings of picnickers
Who were kidnapped by a fright from space.

The crocus bulb stays hidden – veteran
Of terrors beyond man.

### V

Spring bulges the hills.
The bare trees creak and shift.
Some buds have burst in tatters –
Like firework stubs.

But winter's lean bullocks
Only pretend to eat
The grass that will not come.

Then they bound like lambs, they twist in the air
They bounce their half tons of elastic
When the bale of hay breaks open.

They gambol from heap to heap,
Finally stand happy chewing their beards
Of last summer's dusty whiskers.

VI

With arms swinging, a tremendous skater
On the flimsy ice of space,
The earth leans into its curve –

Thrilled to the core, some flies have waded out
An inch onto my window, to stand on the sky
And try their buzz.

## A Swallow

Has slipped through a fracture in the snow-sheet
Which is still our sky –

She flicks past, ahead of her name,
Twinkling away out over the lake.

Reaching this way and that way, with her scissors,
Snipping midges
Trout are still too numb and sunken to stir for.

Sahara clay ovens, at mirage heat,
Glazed her blues, and still she is hot.

She wearied of snatching clegs off the lugs of buffaloes
And of lassooing the flirt-flags of gazelles.

They told her the North was one giant snowball
Rolling South. She did not believe them.
So she exchanged the starry chart of Columbus
For a beggar's bowl of mud.

Setting her compass-tremor tail-needles
She harpooned a wind
That wallowed in the ocean,
Working her barbs deeper
Through that twisting mass she came –

Did she close her eyes and trust in God?
No, she saw lighthouses
Streaming in chaos

Like sparks from a chimney –
She had fixed her instruments on home.

And now, suddenly, into a blanch-tree stillness
A silence of celandines,
A fringing and stupor of frost
She bursts, weightless –
                              to anchor
On eggs frail as frost.

There she goes, flung taut on her leash,
Her eyes at her mouth-corners,
Water-skiing out across a wind
That wrecks great flakes against windscreens.


## April Birthday

When your birthday brings the world under your window
    And the song-thrush sings wet-throated in the dew
And aconite and primrose are unsticking the wrappers
    Of the package that has come today for you

        Lambs bounce out and stand astonished
        Puss willow pushes among bare branches
        Sooty hawthorns shiver into emerald

                    And a new air
            Nuzzles the sugary
            Buds of the chestnut. A groundswell and a stir
            Billows the silvered
            Violet silks
            Of the south – a tenderness
            Lifting through all the
            Gently-breasted
            Counties of England.

When the swallow snips the string that holds the world in
    And the ring-dove claps and nearly loops the loop
You just can't count everything that follows in a tumble
    Like a whole circus tumbling through a hoop

Grass in a mesh of all flowers floundering
Sizzling leaves and blossoms bombing
Nestlings hissing and groggy-legged insects

And the trees
Stagger, they stronger
Brace their boles and biceps under
The load of gift. And the hills float
Light as bubble glass
On the smoke-blue evening

And rabbits are bobbing everywhere, and a thrush
Rings coolly in a far corner. A shiver of green
Strokes the darkening slope as the land
Begins her labour.


## Icecrust and Snowflake

I

A polished glancing. A blue frost-bright dawn.

And the ox's hoof-quag mire
At the ice-cumbered trough has so far protected
A primrose.

And the wild mares, in the moor hollow,
Stand stupid with bliss
Among the first velvet-petalled foal-flowers.

They are weeping for joy in a wind

That blows through the flint of the ox's horn.

II

The North Wind brought you too late

To the iron bar, rusted sodden
In the red soil.

The salmon weightless
In the flag of depth
Green as engine oil.

A snowflake in April
That touched, that registered
Was felt.

Solitary signal
Of a storm too late to get in

Past the iron bar's leaf

Through the window
Of the salmon's egg
With its eager eye.


## Deceptions

The oak is a railway station.
Wait there for the spring.
Will it stop for you?
The famous express blurs through –
Where is it going?
Leaving all the oak's fronds in a blush and agitation –

      Nor will you catch it at the ash.

The March hare brings the spring
For you personally.
He is too drunk to deliver it.
He loses it on some hare-brained folly –
Now you will never recover it.
All year he will be fleeing and flattening his ears and
        fleeing –

      Eluding your fury.

With the cherry bloom for her fancy dress
Spring is giving a party –
And we have been invited.
We've just arrived, all excited,
When she rushes out past us weeping, tattered and dirty –
Wind and rain are wrecking the place

      And we can only go home.

Spring will marry you. A promise!
Cuckoo brings the message: May.
O new clothes! O get your house ready!
Expectation keeps you starry.
But at which church and on what day?
All month you sit waiting, and in June you know that it's
    off.

                And the cuckoo has started to laugh.

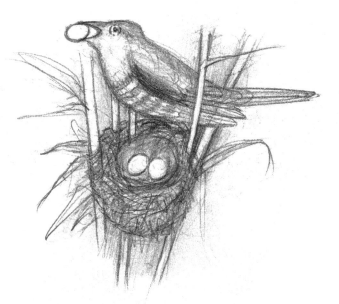

*Summer*

## Swifts

Fifteenth of May. Cherry blossom. The swifts
Materialise at the tip of a long scream
Of needle. 'Look! They're back! Look!' And they're gone
On a steep

Controlled scream of skid
Round the house-end and away under the cherries.
  Gone.
Suddenly flickering in sky summit, three or four together,
Gnat-whisp frail, and hover-searching, and listening

For air-chills – are they too early? With a bowing
Power-thrust to left, then to right, then a flicker they
Tilt into a slide, a tremble for balance,
Then a lashing down disappearance

Behind elms.
            They've made it again,
Which means the globe's still working, the Creation's
Still waking refreshed, our summer's
Still all to come –
               And here they are, here they are again
Erupting across yard stones
Shrapnel-scatter terror. Frog-gapers,
Speedway goggles, international mobsters –

A bolas of three or four wire screams
Jockeying across each other
On their switchback wheel of death.
They swat past, hard-fletched,

Veer on the hard air, toss up over the roof,
And are gone again. Their mole-dark labouring,

Their lunatic limber scramming frenzy
And their whirling blades

Sparkle out into blue –
                    Not ours any more.
Rats ransacked their nests so now they shun us.
Round luckier houses now
They crowd their evening dirt-track meetings,

Racing their discords, screaming as if speed-burned,
Head-height, clipping the doorway
With their leaden velocity and their butterfly lightness,
Their too much power, their arrow-thwack into the eaves.

Every year a first-fling, nearly-flying
Misfit flopped in our yard,
Groggily somersaulting to get airborne.
He bat-crawled on his tiny useless feet, tangling his flails

Like a broken toy, and shrieking thinly
Till I tossed him up – then suddenly he flowed away under
His bowed shoulders of enormous swimming power,
Slid away along levels wobbling

On the fine wire they have reduced life to,
And crashed among the raspberries.
Then followed fiery hospital hours
In a kitchen. The moustached goblin savage

Nested in a scarf. The bright blank
Blind, like an angel, to my meat-crumbs and flies.
Then eyelids resting. Wasted clingers curled.
The inevitable balsa death.

                    Finally burial
For the husk
Of my little Apollo –

The charred scream
Folded in its huge power.

## Mackerel Song

While others sing the mackerel's armour
His stub scissor head and his big blurred eye
And the flimsy savagery of his onset
I sing his simple hunger.

While others sing the mackerel's swagger
His miniature ocelot oil-green stripings
And his torpedo solidity of thump
I sing his gormless plenty.

While others sing the mackerel's fury
The belly-tug lightning-trickle of his evasions
And the wrist-thick muscle of his last word
I sing his loyal come-back.

While others sing the mackerel's acquaintance
The soap of phosphorus he lathers on your fingers
The midget gut and the tropical racer's torso
I sing his scorched sweetness.

While others sing the mackerel's demise
His ultimatum to be cooked instantly
And the shock of his decay announcement
I sing how he makes the rich summer seas

A million times richer

With the gift of his millions.


## Hay

The grass is happy
To run like a sea, to be glossed like a mink's fur
By polishing wind.
Her heart is the weather.
She loves nobody
            Least of all the farmer who leans on the gate.

The grass is happy
When the June sun roasts the foxgloves in the hedges.
She comes into her flower.
She lifts her skirts.
It does not concern her
        The pondering farmer has begun to hope.

The grass is happy
To open her scents, like a dress, through the county,
Drugging light hearts
To heavy betrothals
And next April's Fools,
        While pensioners puzzle where life went so airily.

The grass is happy
When the spinner tumbles her, she silvers and she sweetens.
Plain as a castle
The hare looks for home
And the dusty farmer
        For a hand-shaped cloud and a yellow evening.

Happy the grass
To be wooed by the farmer, who wins her and brings her
   to church in her beauty,
Bride of the Island.
Luckless the long-drawn
Aeons of Eden
        Before he came to mow.


## Evening Thrush

Beyond a twilight of willows and limes
The church craftsman is still busy –
Switing idols,
Rough pre-Goidelic gods and goddesses,
Out of old bits of churchyard yew.

Suddenly flinging
Everything off, head-up, flame-naked,
Plunges shuddering into the creator –

Then comes plodding back, with a limp, over cobbles.

That was a virtuoso's joke.

Now, serious, stretched full height, he aims
At the zenith. He situates a note
Right on the source of light.

Sews a seamless garment, simultaneously
Hurls javelins of dew
Three in air together, catches them.

Explains a studied theorem of sober practicality.

Cool-eyed,
Gossips in a mundane code of splutters
With Venus and Jupiter.
                              Listens –
Motionless, intent astronomer.

Suddenly launches a soul –

The first roses hang in a yoke stupor.
Globe after globe rolls out
Through his fluteful of dew –

The tree-stacks ride out on the widening arc.

Alone and darkening
At the altar of a star
With his sword through his throat
The thrush of clay goes on arguing
Over the graves.

O thrush,
If that really is you, behind the leaf-screen,
Who is this –

Worn-headed, on the lawn's grass, after sunset,
Humped, voiceless, turdus, imprisoned
As a long-distance lorry-driver, dazed

With the pop and static and unending
Of worms and wife and kids?

# Sheep

I

The sheep has stopped crying.
All morning in her wire-mesh compound
On the lawn, she has been crying
For her vanished lamb. Yesterday they came.
Then her lamb could stand, in a fashion,
And make some tiptoe cringing steps.
Now he has disappeared.
He was only half the proper size,
And his cry was wrong. It was not
A dry little hard bleat, a baby-cry
Over a flat tongue, it was human,
It was a despairing human smooth Oh!
Like no lamb I ever heard. Its hindlegs
Cowered in under its lumped spine,
Its feeble hips leaned towards
Its shoulders for support. Its stubby
White wool pyramid head, on a tottery neck,
Had sad and defeated eyes, pinched, pathetic,
Too small, and it cried all the time
Oh! Oh! staggering towards
Its alert, baffled, stamping, storming mother
Who feared our intentions. He was too weak
To find her teats, or to nuzzle up in under,
He hadn't the gumption. He was fully
Occupied just standing, then shuffling
Towards where she'd removed to. She knew
He wasn't right, she couldn't
Make him out. Then his rough-curl legs,
So stoutly built, and hooved
With real quality tips,
Just got in the way, like a loose bundle
Of firewood he was cursed to manage,
Too heavy for him, lending sometimes
Some support, but no strength, no real help.

When we sat his mother on her tail, he mouthed her teat,
Slobbered a little, but after a minute
Lost aim and interest, his muzzle wandered,
He was managing a difficulty
Much more urgent and important. By evening
He could not stand. It was not
That he could not thrive, he was born
With everything but the will –
That can be deformed, just like a limb.
Death was more interesting to him.
Life could not get his attention.
So he died, with the yellow birth-mucus
Still in his cardigan.
He did not survive a warm summer night.
Now his mother has started crying again.
The wind is oceanic in the elms
And the blossom is all set.

II

What is it this time the dark barn again
Where men jerk me off my feet
And shout over me with murder voices
And do something painful to somewhere on my body

Why am I grabbed by the leg and dragged from my friends
Where I was hidden safe though it was hot
Why am I dragged into the light and whirled onto my back
Why am I sat up on my rear end with my legs splayed

A man grips me helpless his knees grip me helpless
What is that buzzer what is it coming
Buzzing like a big fierce insect on a long tangling of snake
What is the man doing to me with his buzzing thing

That I cannot see he is pressing it into me
I surrender I let my legs kick I let myself be killed

I let him hoist me about he twists me flat
In a leverage of arms and legs my neck pinned under his
    ankle

While he does something dreadful down the whole length
    of my belly
My little teats stand helpless and terrified as he buzzes
    around them

Poor old ewe! She peers around from her ridiculous
    position.
Cool intelligent eyes, of grey-banded agate and amber,

Eyes deep and clear with feeling and understanding
While her monster hooves dangle helpless
And a groan like no bleat vibrates in her squashed
    windpipe
And the cutter buzzes at her groin and her fleece piles away

Now it buzzes at her throat and she emerges whitely
More and more grotesquely female and nude
Paunchy and skinny, while her old rug, with its foul tassels
Heaps from her as a foam-stiff, foam-soft, yoke-yellow
    robe

Numbed all over she suddenly feels much lighter
She feels herself free, her legs are her own and she
    scrambles up
Waiting for that grapple of hands to fling her down again
She stands in the opened arch of his knees she is facing a
    bright doorway

With a real bleat to comfort the lamb in herself
She trots across the threshold and makes one high clearing
    bound
To break from the cramp of her fright
And surprised by her new lightness and delighted

She trots away, noble-nosed, her pride unsmirched.
Her greasy winter-weight stays coiled on the foul floor, for
    somebody else to bother about.
She has a beautiful wet green brand on her bobbing brand-
    new backside,
She baas, she has come off best.

The mothers have come back
From the shearing, and behind the hedge
The woe of sheep is like a battlefield
In the evening, when the fighting is over,
And the cold begins, and the dew falls,
And bowed women move with water.
Mother mother mother the lambs
Are crying, and the mothers are crying.
Nothing can resist that probe, that cry
Of a lamb for its mother, or an ewe's crying
For its lamb. The lambs cannot find
Their mothers among those shorn strangers.
A half-hour they have lamented,
Shaking their voices in desperation.
Bald brutal-voiced mothers braying out,
Flat-tongued lambs chopping off hopelessness.
Their hearts are in panic, their bodies
Are a mess of woe, woe they cry,
They mingle their trouble, a music
Of worse and worse distress, a worse entangling,
They hurry out little notes
With all their strength, cries searching this way and that.
The mothers force out sudden despair, blaaa!
On restless feet, with wild heads.

Their anguish goes on and on, in the June heat.
Only slowly their hurt dies, cry by cry,
As they fit themselves to what has happened.


## A Dove

Snaps its twig-tether – mounts –
Dream-yanked up into vacuum
Wings snickering.

Another, in a shatter, hurls dodging away up.

They career through tree-mazes –
Nearly uncontrollable love-weights.

Or now
Temple-dancers, possessed, and steered
By solemn powers
Through insane, stately convulsions.

Porpoises
Of dove-lust and blood-splendour
With arcs
And plungings, and spray-slow explosions.

Now violently gone
Riding the snake of the long love-whip
Among flarings of mares and stallions

Now staying
Coiled on a bough
Bubbling molten, wobbling top-heavy
Into one and many.


## Apple Dumps

After the fiesta, the beauty-contests, the drunken wrestling
Of the blossom
Come some small ugly swellings, the dwarfish truths
Of the prizes.

After blushing and confetti, the breeze-blown bridesmaids,
    the shadowed snapshots
Of the trees in bloom
Come the gruelling knuckles, and the cracked housemaid's
    hands,
The workworn morning plainness of apples.

Unearthly was the hope, the wet star melting the gland,
Staggering the offer –
But pawky the real returns, not easy to see,
Dull and leaf-green, hidden, still-bitter, and hard.

The orchard flared wings, like a new heaven, a
   dawn-lipped apocalypse
Kissing the sleeper –
The apples emerge, in the sun's black shade, among
   stricken trees,
A straggle of survivors, nearly all ailing.


## Work and Play

The swallow of summer, she toils all summer,
A blue-dark knot of glittering voltage,
A whiplash swimmer, a fish of the air.
      But the serpent of cars that crawls through the dust
      In shimmering exhaust
      Searching to slake
      Its fever in ocean
      Will play and be idle or else it will bust.

The swallow of summer, the barbed harpoon,
She flings from the furnace, a rainbow of purples,
Dips her glow in the pond and is perfect.
      But the serpent of cars that collapsed at the beach
      Disgorges its organs
      A scamper of colours
      Which roll like tomatoes
      Nude as tomatoes
      With sand in their creases
      To cringe in the sparkle of rollers and screech.

The swallow of summer, the seamstress of summer,
She scissors the blue into shapes and she sews it,
She draws a long thread and she knots it at corners.
      But the holiday people
      Are laid out like wounded
      Flat as in ovens
      Roasting and basting
      With faces of torment as space burns them blue
      Their heads are transistors
      Their teeth grit on sand grains

Their lost kids are squalling
While man-eating flies
Jab electric shock needles but what can they do?

They can climb in their cars with raw bodies, raw faces
    And start up the serpent
    And headache it homeward
    A car full of squabbles
    And sobbing and stickiness
    With sand in their crannies
    Inhaling petroleum
    That pours from the foxgloves
    While the evening swallow
The swallow of summer, cartwheeling through crimson,
Touches the honey-slow river and turning
Returns to the hand stretched from under the eaves –
A boomerang of rejoicing shadow.


## Hunting the Summer

The fleeing summer! The fleeing summer!
  I got up at dawn,
  In the still, frail dawn
To hunt her and heard the swift's quiver of arrows
    Rattle as she twisted fleeing
      Flying asleep.

The ghostly summer! The ghostly summer!
  Deep was the lane,
  The tarmac velvet,
Banks of cow-parsley brimmed night's creamy stillness,
    Gypsy fox-gloves slept eyes open,
      A field-ghost lingered.

The hot-headed summer! The thoughtless summer!
  A hill in the noon,
  Man-high thistles,
Bullocks that knotted their tails in tight letters
    Bounded rodeo and their roars ripped
      Hanging woodland.

The secret summer! The hiding summer!
    She was sweating a bit
    And a bit too plump
Scarlet she flopped under sycamores panting
        Saying that the butterflies just
            Gave her a headache.

The foxy summer! The swift sly summer!
    On into evening
    I tracked her way
By barley that bowed it and dogrose that littered it,
        Honeysuckle oozing sweetness
            Stopped me dizzied.

Late in the evening I stood by the pond.
Huge was the carp that heaved among big lilies
And sank again, like a whole chest of treasure.
How shall I catch her, the beautiful summer!

I stared at the pond, I stared at the pond
Till the sun slid from my fingertips.
The sun sank under a golden field
And the moon climbed up my back.


## The Harvest Moon

The flame-red moon, the harvest moon,
Rolls along the hills, gently bouncing,
A vast balloon,
Till it takes off, and sinks upward
To lie in the bottom of the sky, like a gold doubloon.

The harvest moon has come,
Booming softly through heaven, like a bassoon.
And earth replies all night, like a deep drum.

So people can't sleep,
So they go out where elms and oak trees keep
A kneeling vigil, in a religious hush.
The harvest moon has come!

And all the moonlit cows and all the sheep
Stare up at her petrified, while she swells
Filling heaven, as if red hot, and sailing
Closer and closer like the end of the world

Till the gold fields of stiff wheat
Cry 'We are ripe, reap us!' and the rivers
Sweat from the melting hills.

## The Golden Boy

In March he was buried
    And nobody cried
Buried in the dirt
    Nobody protested
Where grubs and insects
    That nobody knows
With outer-space faces
    That nobody loves
Can make him their feast
    As if nobody cared.

But the Lord's mother
    Full of her love
Found him underground
    And wrapped him with love
As if he were her baby
    Her own born love
She nursed him with miracles
    And starry love
And he began to live
    And to thrive on her love

He grew night and day
    And his murderers were glad
He grew like a fire
    And his murderers were happy
He grew lithe and tall
    And his murderers were joyful

He toiled in the fields
    And his murderers cared for him
He grew a gold beard
    And his murderers laughed.

With terrible steel
    They slew him in the furrow
With terrible steel
    They beat his bones from him
With terrible steel
    They ground him to powder
They baked him in ovens
    They sliced him on tables
They ate him they ate him
    They ate him they ate him

Thanking the Lord
Thanking the Wheat
Thanking the Bread
For bringing them Life
Today and Tomorrow
Out of the dirt.

*Autumn*

## Leaves

Who's killed the leaves?
Me, says the apple, I've killed them all.
Fat as a bomb or a cannonball
I've killed the leaves.

Who sees them drop?
Me, says the pear, they will leave me all bare
So all the people can point and stare.
I see them drop.

Who'll catch their blood?
Me, me, me, says the marrow, the marrow.
I'll get so rotund that they'll need a wheelbarrow.
I'll catch their blood.

Who'll make their shroud?
Me, says the swallow, there's just time enough
Before I must pack all my spools and be off.
I'll make their shroud.

Who'll dig their grave?
Me, says the river, with the power of the clouds
A brown deep grave I'll dig under my floods.
I'll dig their grave.

Who'll be their parson?
Me, says the Crow, for it is well-known
I study the bible right down to the bone.
I'll be their parson.

Who'll be chief mourner?
Me, says the wind, I will cry through the grass
The people will pale and go cold when I pass.
I'll be chief mourner.

Who'll carry the coffin?
Me, says the sunset, the whole world will weep
To see me lower it into the deep.
I'll carry the coffin.

Who'll sing a psalm?
Me, says the tractor, with my gear grinding glottle
I'll plough up the stubble and sing through my throttle.
I'll sing the psalm.

Who'll toll the bell?
Me, says the robin, my song in October
Will tell the still gardens the leaves are over.
I'll toll the bell.

## The Defenders

With the apple in his strength,
And the quince, his wise adviser,
And the pear his thoughtful brother,
With the blackberry and his thorn,
So ready to shed his blood,
And the plum with his stony bone,
With the wheat in his millions,
The barley and the rye
We shall hold our own
Against all winter's armour.

With the pumpkin in reserve
The turnip and the marrow
We shall hold our fire.
We shall go guerrilla
Asleep among the squirrels.
Over open ground we'll go
In the likeness of a Crow.
When the gale comes we shall claw it
With a claw like a tree,
Then we'll hide down in the roots.
Or in a fox's footprints
Escape across the snow.

And nightly underground
We'll prepare the secret hero,
The little honey bee,
Whose drum, when it begins,
Will bring back all the blossom
And sink the iceberg winter
In the bottom of the sea.

## Autumn Nature Notes

I

The Laburnum top is silent, quite still
In the afternoon yellow September sunlight,
A few leaves yellowing, all its seeds fallen.

Till the goldfinch comes, with a twitching chirrup,
A suddenness, a startlement, at a branch-end.
Then sleek as a lizard, and alert, and abrupt
She enters the thickness, and a machine starts up
Of chitterings, and a tremor of wings, and trillings –
The whole tree trembles and thrills.
It is the engine of her family.
She stokes it full, then flirts out to a branch-end
Showing her barred face identity mask

Then with eerie delicate whistle-chirrup whisperings
She launches away, towards the infinite

And the laburnum subsides to empty.

II

The sun finally tolerable.
The sunflowers tired out, like old gardeners.
Cabbage-white butterflies eddying
In the still pool of what is left to them.
The buddleia's last cones of lilac intoxicant
Crusted with Peacock butterflies and Red Admirals.

A raven, orbiting elm-high, lazily,
Two cronks to each circuit.
Sky sprinkled with forked martins
Swallows glittering their voices.

Now a cooler push, rocking the mesh of soft-edged
    shadows.

So we sit on the earth which is warmed
And sweetened and ripened
By the furnace
On which the door has just about closed.

III

The chestnut splits its padded cell.
It opens an African eye.

A cabinet-maker, an old master
In the root of things, has done it again.

Its slippery gloss is a swoon,
A peek over the edge into – what?

Down the well-shaft of swirly grain,
Past the generous hands that lifted the May-lamps,

Into the Fairytale of a royal tree
That does not know about conkers

Or the war-games of boys.
Invisible though he is, this plump mare

Bears a tall armoured rider towards
The mirk-forest of rooty earth.

He rides to fight the North corner.
He must win a sunbeam princess

From the cloud castle of the rains.
If he fails, evil faces,

Jaws without eyes, will tear him to pieces.
If he succeeds, and has the luck

To snatch his crown from the dragon
Which resembles a slug

He will reign over our garden
For two hundred years.

IV

When the Elm was full
When it heaved and all its tautnesses drummed
Like a full-sail ship

It was just how I felt.
Waist-deep, I ploughed through the lands,
I leaned at horizons, I bore down on strange harbours.

As the sea is a sail-ship's root
So the globe was mine.
When the swell lifted the crow from the Elm-top
Both Poles were my home, they rocked me and supplied me.

But now the Elm is still
All its frame bare
Its leaves are a carpet for the cabbages

And it stands engulfed in the peculiar golden light
With which Eternity's flash
Photographed the sudden cock pheasant –

Engine whinneying, the fire-ball bird clatters up,
Shuddering full-throttle
Its three tongued tail-tip writhing

And the Elm stands, astonished, wet with light,

And I stand, dazzled to my bones, blinded.

V

Through all the orchard's boughs
A honey-colour stillness, a hurrying stealth,
A quiet migration of all that can escape now.

Under ripe apples, a snapshot album is smouldering.

With a bare twig,
Glow-dazed, I coax its stubborn feathers.
A gold furred flame. A blue tremor of the air.

The fleshless faces dissolve, one by one,
As they peel open. Blackenings shrivel
To grey flutter. The clump's core hardens. Everything

Has to be gone through. Every corpuscle
And its gleam. Everything must go.
My heels squeeze wet mulch, and my crouch aches.

A wind-swell lifts through the oak.
Scorch-scathed, crisping, a fleeing bonfire
Hisses in invisible flames – and the flame-roar.

An alarmed blackbird, lean, alert, scolds
The everywhere slow exposure – flees, returns.

VI

Water-wobbling blue-sky-puddled October.
The distance microscopic, the ditches brilliant.
Flowers so low-powered and fractional
They are not in any book.

I walk on high fields feeling the bustle
Of the million earth-folk at their fair.
Fieldfares early, exciting foreigners.
A woodpigeon pressing over, important as a policeman.

A far Bang! Then Bang! and a litter of echoes –
Country pleasures. The farmer's guest,
In U.S. combat green, will be trampling brambles,
Waving his gun like a paddle.

I thought I'd brushed with a neighbour –
Fox-reek, a warm web, rich as creosote,
Draping the last watery blackberries –
But it was the funeral service.

Two nights he has lain, patient in his position,
Puckered under the first dews of being earth,

Crumpled like dead bracken. His reek will cling
To his remains till spring.

Then I shall steal his fangs, and wear them, and honour
them.

VII

Three pale foxglove lamp-mantles, in full flare
Among gritty burned-out spires of old foxgloves
Under needling sleet, in a crossing squall.

This last week, a baby hand of blossom
Among corroded leaves, over windfall apples.

Every apple a festival of small slugs

Probably thinking their good time had just started.

So the old year, tired,
Smiles over his tools, fondling them a little,
As he puts them away.

VIII

Oceanic windy dawn.
Shapes grab at the window.
Ravens go head over heels.
The flood has scoured the sky.

No going on deck today.
I see, through the submerged window,
That the quince tree, which yesterday
Still clung to a black leaf, has lost it.

## The Seven Sorrows

The first sorrow of autumn
Is the slow goodbye
Of the garden who stands so long in the evening –
A brown poppy head,
The stalk of a lily,
And still cannot go.

The second sorrow
Is the empty feet
Of the pheasant who hangs from a hook with his brothers.
The woodland of gold
Is folded in feathers
With its head in a bag.

And the third sorrow
Is the slow goodbye
Of the sun who has gathered the birds and who gathers
The minutes of evening,
The golden and holy
Ground of the picture.

The fourth sorrow
Is the pond gone black
Ruined and sunken the city of water –
The beetle's palace,
The catacombs
Of the dragonfly.

And the fifth sorrow
Is the slow goodbye
Of the woodland that quietly breaks up its camp.
One day it's gone.
It has left only litter –
Firewood, tentpoles.

And the sixth sorrow
Is the fox's sorrow
The joy of the huntsman, the joy of the hounds,
The hooves that pound
Till earth closes her ear
To the fox's prayer.

And the seventh sorrow
Is the slow goodbye
Of the face with its wrinkles that looks through the window
As the year packs up
Like a tatty fairground
That came for the children.

# The Stag

While the rain fell on the November woodland shoulder of
    Exmoor
While the traffic jam along the road honked and shouted
Because the farmers were parking wherever they could
And scrambling to the bank-top to stare through the
    tree-fringe
Which was leafless,
The stag ran through his private forest.

While the rain drummed on the roofs of the parked cars
And kids inside cried and daubed their chocolate and fought
And mothers and aunts and grandmothers
Were a tangle of undoing sandwiches and screwed-round
    gossiping heads
Steaming up the windows,
The stag loped through his favourite valley.

While the blue horsemen down in the boggy meadow
Sodden nearly black, on sodden horses,
Spaced as at a military parade,
Moved a few paces to the right and a few to the left and
    felt rather foolish
Looking at the brown impassable river,
The stag came over the last hill of Exmoor.

While everybody high-kneed it to the bank-top all along
    the road
Where steady men in oilskins were stationed at binoculars,
And the horsemen down by the river galloped anxiously
    this way and that
And the cry of hounds came tumbling invisibly with their
    echoes down through the draggle of trees,
Swinging across the wall of dark woodland,
The stag dropped into a strange country.

And turned at the river
Hearing the hound-pack smash the undergrowth, hearing
    the bell-note

Of the voice that carried all the others,
Then while his limbs all called different directions to his
    lungs, which only wanted to rest,
The blue horsemen on the bank opposite
Pulled aside the camouflage of their terrible planet.

And the stag doubled back weeping and looking for home
    up a valley and down a valley
While the strange trees struck at him and the brambles
    lashed him,
And the strange earth came galloping after him carrying the
    loll-tongued hounds to fling all over him
And his heart became just a club beating his ribs and his
    own hooves shouted with hounds' voices,
And the crowd on the road got back into their cars
Wet-through and disappointed.


## Two Horses

### I

Earth heaved, splitting. Towers
Reared out. I emerged
Behind horses, updragging with oaken twists
Swaying castles of elastic

My fortifications moved on the sky
The ploughshare my visor
Crowned by wind burn, ploughing my kingdom

Instated by the sun's sway
The fortunes of war, a famished people
Corn barons.

### II

I advanced
Under the November sooty gold heaven
Among angling gulls

Behind those earth-swaying buttocks
Their roil and gleam, as in a dark wind

And the smoky foliage of their labour
Their tree-strength

Hauling earth's betrothal
From an underworld, with crocus glints
A purplish cloak-flap
The click hooves flicking
Hot circles flashing back at me lightly

Shaggy forest giants, gentle in harness
Their roots tearing and snapping
They were themselves the creaking boughs and the burden
Of earth's fleshiest ripeness, her damson tightest
Her sweetest

Earth splayed her thighs, she lay back.

III

The coulter slid effortless
The furrow's polished face, with a hiss
Coiling aside, a bow-wave that settled
Beside the poisonous brown river
As I stumbled deeper.
                              Hour after hour
The tall sweat-sleeked buttocks
Mill-wheels heavily revolving
Slackness to tautness, stretch and quiver – the vein-mapped
Watery quake-weight
In their slapping traces, drawing me deeper

Into the muffled daze and toil of their flames
Their black tails slashing sideways
The occasional purring snort

The stubble's brassy whisper
The mineral raw earth smell, the town-wind of sulphur
The knotted worms, sheared by light
The everlasting war behind the shoulder
The old ploughman still young

Furrow by furrow darkening toward summer.

IV

A shout – and the dream broke, against the thorns of the
   headland.
Chins back, backing
Trampling sideways, a jangling of brisk metals
High-kneed, levered by cries
The plough hard over –

They had jerked awake
Into urgent seconds
Now they trod deep water, champing foam
Where were they suddenly?
                                   And suddenly they knew

Like turning in a bed, and settling to sleep
The share sank

With a hard sigh, the furrow-slice sprawled over

And they bowed again to their worship.


V

The last friendly angels
Lifting their knees out of the earth, their clay-balled
   fetlocks
Heads down praying

And lifting me with them, into their furnace

I walked in their flames

Their long silk faces, shag-haired as old sheepdogs
Their brown eyes, like prehistoric mothers
Their mouse-belly mouths, their wire-spring whiskers
Sudden yellow teeth of the nightmare and skull

Wading the earth's wealth
In a steam of dung and sweat, to soft horse-talk

Nodding and slow in their power, climbing the sky

On the crumbling edge.

# A Cranefly in September

She is struggling through grass-mesh – not flying,
Her wide-winged, stiff, weightless basket-work of limbs
Rocking, like an antique wain, a top-heavy ceremonial cart
Across mountain summits
(Not planing over water, dipping her tail)
But blundering with long strides, long reachings, reelings
And ginger-glistening wings
From collision to collision.
Aimless in no particular direction,
Just exerting her last to escape out of the overwhelming
Of whatever it is, legs, grass,
The garden, the county, the country, the world –

Sometimes she rests long minutes in the grass forest
Like a fairytale hero, only a marvel can help her.
She cannot fathom the mystery of this forest
In which, for instance, this giant watches –
The giant who knows she cannot be helped in any way.

Her jointed bamboo fuselage,
Her lobster shoulders, and her face
Like a pinhead dragon, with its tender moustache,
And the simple colourless church windows of her wings
Will come to an end, in mid-search, quite soon.
Everything about her, every perfected vestment
Is already superfluous.
The monstrous excess of her legs and curly feet
Are a problem beyond her.
The calculus of glucose and chitin inadequate
To plot her through the infinities of the stems.

The frayed apple leaves, the grunting raven, the defunct
    tractor
Sunk in nettles, wait with their multiplications
Like other galaxies.
The sky's Northward September procession, the vast soft
    armistice,

Like an Empire on the move,
Abandons her, tinily embattled
With her cumbering limbs and cumbered brain.

## There Came a Day

There came a day that caught the summer
Wrung its neck
Plucked it
And ate it.

Now what shall I do with the trees?
The day said, the day said.
Strip them bare, strip them bare.
Let's see what is really there.

And what shall I do with the sun?
The day said, the day said.
Roll him away till he's cold and small.
He'll come back rested if he comes back at all.

And what shall I do with the birds?
The day said, the day said.
The birds I've frightened, let them flit,
I'll hang out pork for the brave tomtit.

And what shall I do with the seed?
The day said, the day said.
Bury it deep, see what it's worth.
See if it can stand the earth.

What shall I do with the people?
The day said, the day said.
Stuff them with apple and blackberry pie –
They'll love me then till the day they die.

There came this day and he was autumn.
His mouth was wide
And red as a sunset.
His tail was an icicle.

# Barley

Barley grain is like seeds of gold bullion.
When you turn a heap with a shovel it pours
With the heavy magic of wealth.
Every grain is a sleeping princess –
Her kingdom is still to come.
She sleeps with sealed lips.
Each grain is like a mouth sealed
Or an eye sealed.
In each mouth the whole bible of barley.
In each eye, the whole sun of barley.
From each single grain, given time,
You could feed the earth.

You treat them rough, dump them into the drill,
Churn them up with a winter supply
Of fertiliser, and steer out onto the tilth
Trailing your wake of grains.

When the field's finished, fresh-damp,
Its stillness is no longer stillness.
The coverlet has been drawn tight again
But now over breathing and dreams.
And water is already bustling to sponge the newcomers.
And the soil, the ancient nurse,
Is assembling everything they will need.
And the angel of earth
Is flying through the field, kissing each one awake.
But it is a hard nursery.
Night and day all through winter huddling naked
They have to listen to pitiless lessons
Of the freezing constellations
And the rain. If it were not for the sun
Who visits them daily, briefly,
To pray with them, they would lose hope
And give up. With him
They recite the Lord's prayer
And sing a psalm. And sometimes at night

When the moon haunts their field and stares down
Into their beds
They sing a psalm softly together
To keep up their courage.

Once their first leaf shivers they sing less
And start working. They cannot miss a day.
They have to get the whole thing right.
Employed by the earth, employed by the sky,
Employed by barley, to be barley.
And now they begin to show their family beauty.
They come charging over the field, under the wind, like
    warriors –
'Terrible as an army with banners',
Barbaric, tireless, Amazon battalions.

And that's how they win their kingdom.
Then they put on gold, for their coronation.
Each one barbed, feathered, a lithe weapon,
Puts on the crown of her kingdom.
Then the whole fieldful of queens
Swirls in a dance
With their invisible partner, the wind,
Like a single dancer.

That is how barley inherits the kingdom of barley.

*Winter*

## Pets

A dark November night, late. The back door wide.
Beyond the doorway, the step off into space.
On the threshold, looking out,
With foxy-furry tail lifted, a kitten.
Somewhere out there, a badger, our lodger,
A stripe-faced rusher at cats, a grim savager,
Is crunching the bones and meat of a hare
Left out for her nightly emergence
From under the outhouses.

The kitten flirts his tail, arches his back –
All his hairs are inquisitive.
Dare he go for a pee?
Something is moving there, just in dark.
A prowling lump. Grows. A tabby tom.
And the battered master of the house
After a month at sea, comes through the doorway.

Recovered from his nearly fatal mauling,
Two, probably three pounds heavier
Since that last time he dragged in for help.
He deigns to recognise me
With his criminal eyes, his deformed voice.
Then poises, head lowered, muscle-bound,
Like a bull for the judges,
A thick Devon bull,
Sniffing the celebration of sardines.

## The Warrior of Winter

He met the star his enemy
    They fought the woods leafless.

237

He gripped his enemy.
   They trampled fields to quag.
His enemy was stronger.
   A star fought against him.

He fought his losing fight
   Up to the neck in the river.
Grimly he fought in gateways,
   He struggled among stones.
He left his strength in puddles.
   The star grew stronger.

Rising and falling
   He blundered against houses.
He gurgled for life in ditches.
   Clouds mopped his great wounds.
His shattered weapons glittered.
   The star gazed down.

Wounded and prisoner
   He slept on rotten sacking.
He gnawed bare stalks and turnip tops
   In the goose's field.
The sick sheep froze beside him.
   The star was his guard.

With bones like frozen plumbing
   He lay in the blue morning.
His teeth locked in his head
   Like the trap-frozen fox.
But he rejoiced a tear in the sun.
   Like buds his dressings softened.


## Starlings Have Come

A horde out of sub-Arctic Asia
Darkening nightfall, a faint sky-roar
Of pressure on the ear.

More thicken the vortex, gloomier.

A bacteria cyclone, a writhing of imps
Issuing from a hole in the horizon
Topples and blackens a whole farm.

Now a close-up seething of fleas.
                              And now a silence –
The doom-panic mob listens, for a second.
Then, with a soft boom, they wrap you
Into their mind-warp, assembling a nightmare sky-wheel
Of escape – a Niagara
Of upward rumbling wings – that collapses again

In an unmanageable weight
Of neurotic atoms.
                    They're the subconscious
Of the Smart-Alec, all slick hair and Adam's apple,
Sunday chimney starling.
                         This Elizabethan songster,
Italianate, in damask, emblematic,
Trembles his ruff, pierces the Maytime
With his perfected whistle
Of a falling bomb – or frenzies himself
Into a Gothic, dishevelled madness,
Chattering his skeleton, sucking his brains,
Gargling his blood through a tin flute –
                              Ah, Shepster!
Suddenly such a bare dagger of listening!

Next thing – down at the bread
Screeching like a cat
Limber and saurian on your hind legs,

Tumbling the sparrows with a drop kick –

A Satanic hoodlum, a cross-eyed boss,
Black body crammed with hot rubies
And Anthrax under your nails.

## Christmas Card

You have anti-freeze in the car, yes,
    But the shivering stars wade deeper.
Your scarf's tucked in under your buttons,
    But a dry snow ticks through the stubble.
Your knee-boots gleam in the fashion,
    But the moon must stay

        And stamp and cry
        As the holly the holly
        Hots its reds.

Electric blanket to comfort your bedtime
    The river no longer feels its stones.
Your windows are steamed by dumpling laughter
    The snowplough's buried on the drifted moor.
Carols shake your television
    And nothing moves on the road but the wind

        Hither and thither
        The wind and three
        Starving sheep.

Redwings from Norway rattle at the clouds
    But comfortless sneezers puddle in pubs.
The robin looks in at the kitchen window
    But all care huddles to hearths and kettles.
The sun lobs one wet snowball feebly
    Grim and blue

        The dusk of the coombe
        And the swamp woodland
        Sinks with the wren.

See old lips go purple and old brows go paler.
    The stiff crow drops in the midnight silence.
Sneezes grow coughs and coughs grow painful.
    The vixen yells in the midnight garden.
You wake with the shakes and watch your breathing
    Smoke in the moonlight – silent, silent.

Your anklebone
And your anklebone
Lie big in the bed.

## December River

After the brown harvest of rains, express lights
Are riding behind bare poles.

As the flood clears to cider and shrinks a little,
Leaves spinning and toiling in the underboil,
I go to find salmon.

A frost-fragility hangs.
Duck-eggshell emptiness, bare to the space-freeze.
Jupiter crucified and painful. Vapour-trails keen as incisions.

Blackly
Crusty tricorne sycamore leaves are tick-tocking down
To hit the water with a hard tiny crash.

From under the slag-smoke west
The molten river comes, bulging,
With its skin of lights.

Too late now to see much
I wade into the unfolding metals.

This vein from the sky is the sea-spirit's pathway.

Here all year salmon have been their own secret.
They were the heavy slipperiness in the green oils.

The steady name – unfathomable –
In the underbrow stare-darkness.

They leapfrogged the river's fifty-mile ladder
With love-madness for strength,
Weightlifting through all its chimneys of tonnage

And came to their never-never land – to these
Gutters the breadth of a tin bath.
And dissolved

Into holes of obviousness. Anchored in strongholds
Of a total absence. Became
The transparency of their own windows.

So, day in day out, this whole summer
I offered all I had for a touch of their wealth –
I found only endlessly empty water.

But I go now, in near-darkness,
Frost, and close to Christmas, and am admitted
To glance down and see, right at my heel,
A foot under, where backwater mills rubbish,
Like a bleached hag laid out – the hooked gape
And gargoyle lobster-claw grab

Of a dead salmon, and its white shirt-button eye.

That grimace
Of getting right through to the end and beyond it –
That helm
So marvellously engineered

Discarded, an empty stencil.
A negative, pale
In the dreggy swirlings
Of earth's already beginning mastication.

I freed it, I wanted to get it
Wedged properly mine
While the moment still held open.

As I lifted its child-heavy rubbery bulk
Marbled crimson like an old woman's fire-baked thigh

The shallows below lifted
A broad bow-wave lifted and came frowning
Straight towards me, setting the whole pool rocking,

And slid under smoothness into the trench at my feet.

Into the grave of steel
Which it could still buckle.

# New Year Song

Now there comes
  The Christmas rose
    But that is eerie
        too like a ghost
   Too like a creature
        preserved under glass
   A blind white fish
        from an underground lake
   Too like last year's widow
       at a window
       And the worst cold's to come.

Now there comes
  The tight-vest lamb
   With its wriggle eel tail
       and its wintry eye
   With its ice-age mammoth
       unconcern
   Letting the aeon
       seconds go by
   With its little peg hooves
       to dot the snow
   Following its mother
       into worse cold and worse
       And the worst cold's to come.

Now there come
  The weak-neck snowdrops
   Bouncing like fountains
       and they stop you, they make you
   Take a deep breath
       make your heart shake you
   Such a too much of a gift
       for such a mean time
   Nobody knows
       how to accept them

All you can do
          is gaze at them baffled
          And the worst cold's to come.

And now there comes
  The brittle crocus
    To be nibbled by the starving hares
          to be broken by snow
    Now comes the aconite
          purpled by cold
    A song comes into
          the storm-cock's fancy
    And the robin and the wren
          they rejoice like each other
    In an hour of sunlight
          for something important
          Though the worst cold's to come.


## Snow and Snow

Snow is sometimes a she, a soft one.
  Her kiss on your cheek, her finger on your sleeve
In early December, on a warm evening,
  And you turn to meet her, saying 'It's snowing!'
    But it is not. And nobody's there.
    Empty and calm is the air.

Sometimes the snow is a he, a sly one.
  Weakly he signs the dry stone with a damp spot.
Waifish he floats and touches the pond and is not.
  Treacherous-beggarly he falters, and taps at the window.
    A little longer he clings to the grass-blade tip
    Getting his grip.

Then how she leans, how furry foxwrap she nestles
  The sky with her warm, and the earth with her softness.
How her lit crowding fairytales sink through the space-
    silence
  To build her palace, till it twinkles in starlight –

Too frail for a foot
Or a crumb of soot.

Then how his muffled armies move in all night
And we wake and every road is blockaded
Every hill taken and every farm occupied
And the white glare of his tents is on the ceiling.
And all that dull blue day and on into the gloaming
We have to watch more coming.

Then everything in the rubbish-heaped world
Is a bridesmaid at her miracle.
Dunghills and crumbly dark old barns are bowed in the
chapel of her sparkle,
The gruesome boggy cellars of the wood
Are a wedding of lace
Now taking place.


## The Warm and the Cold

Freezing dusk is closing
Like a slow trap of steel
On trees and roads and hills and all
That can no longer feel.
But the carp is in its depth
Like a planet in its heaven.
And the badger in its bedding
Like a loaf in the oven.
And the butterfly in its mummy
Like a viol in its case.
And the owl in its feathers
Like a doll in its lace.

Freezing dusk has tightened
Like a nut screwed tight
On the starry aeroplane
Of the soaring night.
But the trout is in its hole
Like a chuckle in a sleeper.
The hare strays down the highway

Like a root going deeper.
The snail is dry in the outhouse
Like a seed in a sunflower.
The owl is pale on the gatepost
Like a clock on its tower.

Moonlight freezes the shaggy world
Like a mammoth of ice –
The past and the future
Are the jaws of a steel vice.
But the cod is in the tide-rip
Like a key in a purse.
The deer are on the bare-blown hill
Like smiles on a nurse.
The flies are behind the plaster
Like the lost score of a jig.
Sparrows are in the ivy-clump
Like money in a pig.

Such a frost
The flimsy moon
Hast lost her wits.

A star falls.

The sweating farmers
Turn in their sleep
Like oxen on spits.

# Very New Foal

         The moorland mother's
Dirty white. Perfunctory
She goes on shortening the short grass,
Leaning onto her nibble, at the road's edge
With a few other new mothers. Sun
Comes down warm, through the hard wind
That goes over the ridge.
                 The new foal
Is dirtier than his mother. Maybe
He'll grow to be a dappled grey. Maybe not.
At the moment he's not much of anything.
He's up and spellbound, hanging his head
Which is still womb-rounded, primeval
Lizard shoe-shaped, not noble bony
Or stress-delicate horse-like, or alert
Lifted into the trembling fringe of senses,
But sleepy, terribly sleepy, eyes
Just glad to sink back dozy, head
Hanging in mother-comfort, fringed with sun-glow,
The dainty curl of beard in sun-glow,
Drying out, and the knotty plait of mane
Drying out, and the knotty, twisty
Plait of tail drying to looseness. He leans
Onto his shoulders, stretching
His embryo curve straight, reflexing
The new soft bow of his spine,
And his hind-knees lean together,
Taking a rest one against the other
Even as he stretches. He positions
His front legs, discovering
How tables stay steady. He dozes
There in mid-stretch, slackening,
His head hanging, tired with surprise,
His nose hanging out there, heavy,
In front of his eyes.

UNCOLLECTED

Others
Not much older, only hours older,
Sit like little horses, near mothers,
Legs cleverly folded already
Tightly compact, keeping the world out,
But their necks up, and arched
Like the necks of sea-horses, and their heads
Bowed at just that angle. Just the angle,
Half-sleep and half-pride, of swans
Shouldering their splendour along,
Breasting the world-surge, hanging in sleep,
Slightly tucked-in chins, like sea-horses,
Such a sleepy, poised angle. A pose
Brought from the other world, a deeper place
Where Seraphim surge in sleep-stillness,
Breasting waves of light, their eyes
Lowered, their brows
Fronting the source, the bulging towards them
Of the world, the world's hum, the small cries.


## A Lamb in the Storm

But the world is brave.
Eyes squeezed tight shut, she plunges.
Surf goes over the house, dust-bin lids fly.

Ears of owls, hairfine electronics
Are jammed with the sky-disaster.
They anchor their cork-weights, clamped hungry
To trees that struggle to save themselves.

The world's brow
Plunges into blindness and deafness –
Farms and villages cling.

Chunks of the wreck reel past.

But the world
Just about finished,
Stripped and stunned, keeps her battered direction –

She knows who it is, still alive out there,
That castaway voice
Where heaven breaks up in the darkness.

# Index of Titles

251

# Index of First Lines

My Uncle Mick the portrait artist painted Nature's Creatures, 49

Nasturtiums on earth are small and seething with horrible green caterpillars, 80
No feet. Snow, 122
No, it is not an elephant or any such grasshopper, 57
Now let's have another try, 24
Now the river is rich, but her voice is low, 196
Now there comes, 243

O early one dawn I walked over the dew, 188
O he steals our crooked speeches, says the Hunting Horn, 172
O hear the Whale's, 14
'O see my eyes', 14
O the White-Collared Dove has a swollen nose, 164
Ocean's huge hammer, 5
On a tree-bole, a zigzag upward rivulet, 159
On the moon lives an eye, 97
On the moon with great ease, 89
On the whole, people dislike spiders, 190
Once I crept in an oakwood – I was looking for a stag, 52
Once upon a time there was a person, 107
One time we had nothing else of course and handsome they were, 142
Owl! Owl, 30

People on the moon love a pet, 96
Pets are the Hobby of my brother Bert, 45
Pigeons! They're problems. You know why their crop's called a crop, 157

Ragworm once, 8
Right from the start he is dressed in his best – his blacks and his whites, 195
Rooks love excitement. When I walked in under the rookery, 145

Saddest of all things on the moon is the snail without a shell, 83
Set the stage, 72
She grin-lifts, 127
She is struggling through grass-mesh – not flying, 233
Shining like lamps and light as balloons, 81
Shrill and astonishing the shrew, 30
Sing the hole's plume, the rafter's cockade, 143
Singing on the moon seems precarious, 106
Skunk's footfall plods padded, 123
Snaps its twig-tether – mounts, 214
Snow is sometimes a she, a soft one, 244
So I run out. I am holding a hare, 105
Some fathers work at the office, others work at the store, 51
Some people on the moon are so idle, 101
Sparrow squats in the dust, 29

That Elf, 176
The Badger in the spinney is the true king of this land, 137
The Bear's black bulk, 113
The beggarly Bat, a cut-out, scattily, 149
The Brooktrout, superb as a matador, 119
The Cow comes home swinging, 23
The Cow is but a bagpipe, 140
The Crow is a wicked creature, 35
The Cuckoo's the crookedest, wickedest bird, 32
The fierce Osprey, 121
The first sorrow of autumn, 227